Glitz and Glam
2302 Valley View West
Pleasant Hill, MO 64080
Phone 816-898-8831

D1517596

Order Form

NAME_____

Phone#_____

If you are adding your name to your shirt, please PRINT your name clearly below. No refunds will be made for misspelled names.

Name_____

DESIGN TO BE PLACED ON CHEST AT THE: (CIRCLE ONE)

Right   **Left**   **Center**

SALESPERSON	P.O. NUMBER	REQUISITIONER	SHIPPED VIA	F.O.B. POINT	TERMS
Angela Allard	Twilight Stitchers Quilt Guild	Blue Springs	N/A	N/A	Due at order

DESIGN $17.00	NAME $3.00	UNIT PRICE	TOTAL
1 shirt	Angela Allard EXAMPLE	$20.00	$20.00
		SUBTOTAL	
		SALES TAX 9.5%	
		TOTAL DUE	

Make all checks payable to: **Angela Allard**
Please attach your completed order form to your shirt/shirts (perhaps putting them in a baggie along with your check).

Thank you for your business!

Beyond the Basics

A Potpourri of Quiltmaking Techniques

by Kathy Delaney

Sheila — Go Beyond the Basics!
Kathy Delaney

Kansas City Star Books

Beyond the Basics:
A Potpourri of Quiltmaking Techniques

By Kathy Delaney

Edited by Judy Pearlstein
Tech edited by Deb McCurnin
Design by Cheryl Johnson, S&Co. Design, Inc.
Quilt Photographs by Aaron Leimkuehler
Instructional Photos by Kathy Delaney
Illustrations by Lon Eric Craven
Production Assistance by Jo Ann Groves

Published by Kansas City Star Books
1729 Grand Boulevard
Kansas City, Missouri 64108

First edition, first printing
ISBN: 978-1-933466-35-4

Printed in the United States of America
By Walsworth Publishing Co.
Marceline, Missouri

To order copies, call StarInfo, 816-234-4636
(Say "Operator.")

KANSAS CITY STAR BOOKS

www.Pickledish.com http://www.pickledish.com/

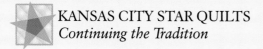 KANSAS CITY STAR QUILTS
Continuing the Tradition

 PickleDish.com
The Quilter's Home Page

Kathy cannot remember when she wasn't sewing. Starting with doll clothes and graduating to her own clothes by the time she was ten, Kathy has had a love affair with fabric that has never diminished.

Since meeting her first quilt in 1991, Kathy has moved away from clothing almost entirely and has devoted her creative endeavors to the making of quilts. In fact, on any given day, she can be found thinking about her next quilt, shopping for fabric for a new quilt, stitching on a current quilt, writing about quiltmaking techniques, designing patterns for quilters, sketching ideas for another appliqué quilt, taking a workshop to learn a new technique, attending a guild meeting, lecturing or teaching quiltmaking techniques. In fact, her husband does not believe she does anything but make quilts. He just might be right!

Kathy lives in Overland Park, Kansas with Rich, her husband of 35 years. She and her husband have two sons, Sean, 26, just returned from two tours in Iraq and now a civilian, and Ian, 22, an actor living in North Hollywood. Kathy and Rich also have their first and second grandchildren, twins, born to Sean and his wife Alicia.

Kathy is available to travel for guild programs, workshops and judging. She may be contacted through her website, www.kathydelaney.com.

Introduction

Beyond the Basics – A Potpourri of Quiltmaking Techniques

When I wrote "The Basics – an Easy Guide to Beginning Quiltmaking"
I always planned to expand on the skills described for the sampler quilt
and take the beginning quiltmaker to the next level. I tried very hard to
come up with a theme for this new collection of skills and patterns and
discovered there really isn't anything that ties each of the patterns to
all the others. But I did think of the collection as a *potpourri* – a French
word for a fragrant mixture of flower petals and spices used to scent
the air. Loosely, a potpourri of quiltmaking skills is a sweet mixture of
techniques to make your quiltmaking easier or more successful.

Potpourri turns out to be a musical term, too. The term is usually
applied to a composition that consists of a string of favorite tunes or
a collection of songs, familiarly, a medley. It is my hope that the
collection of quiltmaking techniques offered on the following pages
becomes a medley you will enjoy in all your quilting projects.

I include a variety of techniques – paper foundation piecing,
Y-seams, isosceles triangle unit, designing beyond the block,
60-degree diamonds, curved piecing, machine and hand
appliqué – all designed to increase your quiltmaking skills. You
don't have to make the projects in any order. One skill set does
not necessarily build upon the other. Just have fun!

Acknowledgements

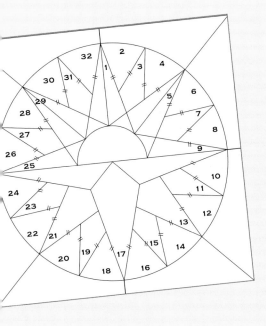

One of the things I was reminded of while writing this book is how important good friends are. Good friends do more than caress your soul. They also help when a project seems overwhelming. I began writing this book by designing a collection of patterns, incorporating some of my favorite techniques. The thought of my making all of the quilts I had designed in the time I had to do it became quite overwhelming. When my friends began offering to make the quilts for me, thus testing the patterns, I counted myself very lucky indeed. Following are the friends who truly made this project happen: in alphabetical order, I thank Kelly Ashton, Barb Fife, Natalie Hutchison, Tresa Jones, Nancy Khu, Cindy Miller, Linda Mooney, Kim Morrow, Jeanne Poore, and the machine quilters, Alice Scott, Freda Smith and Lynne Zeh. I'd like to mention that some of the quilters who tested the pattern and made the samples found on thesae pages were new to the techniques described. Being inexperienced in the methods certainly did not keep them from making the wonderful quilts you see. I hope you are encouraged by their success!

Speaking of friends – it was nice to once again be working with Judy Pearlstein, editor of "The Basics" and Jo Ann Groves, who always makes sure the color is right. Thank you, Judy and Jo Ann, for all your help! I'd like to thank new friends, Cheryl Johnson, the designer of this book and Deb McCurnin, who checked all the technical stuff. And thank you, Aaron Leimkuhler, for the photography and Lon Eric Craven for the graphics. Finally, I would like to thank my daughter-in-law, Alicia Delaney, for helping me with my final instructional photograph. I couldn't have done it without her!

I'm grateful for Doug Weaver's faith. I appreciate his support in my addiction in regards to teaching. The books I write for *Kansas City Star Books* let me reach the longest list of students!

And last, but certainly not least, I thank you, the reader, for your faith in me by buying this book. May you go beyond the basics in your quiltmaking!

Table of Contents

Second seam

Stop stitching 1/4" from the corner in the inside corner

Third seam

This is 3/8"

The seam allowance is 1/4" from the raw edge.

4

3

1

5

2

6

Freezer Paper Foundation Piecing

These simple directions for paper foundation piecing are very similar to what you have been doing as you foundation pieced on paper. The difference is you will not be sewing through the paper on the line. Instead, you will be sewing right next to the line. The paper is folded back on the line so when you sew you will not be catching the paper. The advantage is you will not have to tear the paper away when your block is complete. Merely peel the paper away. In addition, the paper pattern is reusable.

Cut fabric for individual patches

Set your ruler over the patch. Allow 1/2" all around. Cut a square or a rectangle; in this case you won't need to consider the grain line. The outside edges of the block will, for the most part, be on grain.

Sewing fabric with the paper foundation pattern

Place #1 fabric behind the pattern, wrong side of fabric to shiny side of paper and press with dry iron set on wool.

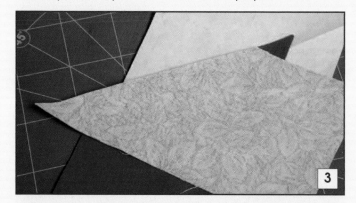

Fold the pattern back on the line between patches #1 and #2 (1). Trim 1/4" seam allowance using an Add-a-Quarter ruler and a 28 mm rotary cutter. (2)

Align the fabric for patch #2 to the just-cut edge (3); sew right next to the folded paper. (4) Press the fabric pieces open and to freezer paper.

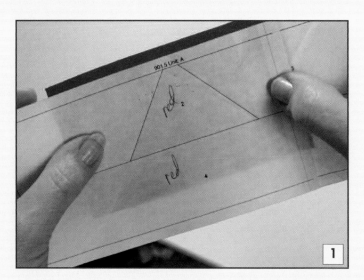

Fold the pattern back on the line between patch #3 and the sewn unit. Trim 1/4" seam allowance.

Align the fabric for patch #3 to the just-cut edge; sew right next to the folded paper. Press the fabric open and to the freezer paper.

Fold the pattern back on the line between patch #4 and the sewn unit. Trim 1/4" seam allowance.

Align the fabric for patch #4 to the just-cut edge and sew next to the folded paper. Press the fabric open and to the freezer paper.

When all of the patches are sewn and pressed to the freezer paper, trim around the block, adding a 1/4" seam allowance. Carefully peel the paper pattern from the back of the block. If you have bias edges you may want to leave the pattern on the block until you set the blocks into the quilt top. In this case you will need a pattern for each block. To remove the paper, slide a pin or stiletto between the paper and the fabric to release the paper. The freezer paper pattern may be reused if the edges were not caught in the seam.

Curved Piecing

As with most techniques in quiltmaking, there is no one way to accomplish the curved seam. Some people support pinning, while others don't bother. Some people clip before stitching while others clip after. There is even a special foot to put on your sewing machine to aid in piecing curved edges. So on these pages I will give you directions for how I piece two curved seams.

When I refer to curved piecing, I am referring to sewing arcs, a "valley" sewn to a "hill," if you will. Most often you will find this manifested in the shape of 1/4 of a circle sewn into a square as for the Drunkard's Path block.

If you have acrylic templates for the shapes, you can use your small (28 mm) rotary cutter to cut your fabric shapes. However, without the presence of the acrylic templates you'll have to use scissors, but pinning paper templates in place and cutting around them can allow distortion. I would recommend using a template plastic or, better yet, freezer paper, to trace the provided template directly onto the fabric and cutting it out very carefully. (5)

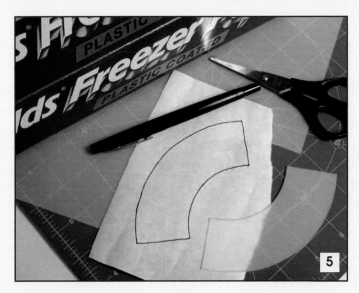

Begin by stabilizing your fabric. Heavily starch the fabric and press. The starch will help the fabric maintain its shape as you work, keeping your blocks from distorting.

Trace the template, 1/4" seam allowance included, onto the paper side of freezer paper and cut out. (If you were to be hand piecing, the template would not include the seam allowance. The line you trace would be the stitching line.) Press the paper template onto your fabric, right or wrong side, with a dry iron set on the wool setting. (If you were to be hand piecing, you would want the traced line on the wrong side of the fabric.) With a fabric marker, light for dark fabric and dark for light fabric, trace the template. Using sharp scissors, cut out the shape using the traced line as your guide. Cut right on the line or right next to the inside edge of the line. Cutting one layer of fabric at a time is the most accurate. You probably can cut two layers at a time if you pin the layers to stabilize. Any more than two, though, will probably result in misshapen arcs.

There is a way of using a rotary cutter and ruler to cut the fabric. It involves moving the ruler along the outside edge of the curved edge of the template as you move the rotary cutter along the edge of the ruler. It takes some practice, but you can do it. The straight edges are easy. (6)

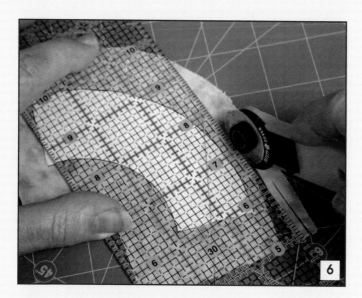

To sew the two parts together, begin by finding the center of both arcs. I just fold the arc in half and pinch the seam allowance at the fold to mark.(7)

Repeat with the other piece. (8) With right sides together, match the center mark on both pieces and place a pin to hold. I always place the "hill" on the bottom and pin the "valley" to it to sew. Align the ends and pin together. That's all it takes: 3 pins. If it is a very large block, more pins are desired. Find the center of one half of the arcs, again by pinching the folds, and pin. Keep finding the center and pinching to mark.

As you sew, the hill will remain flat as it passes over the feed dogs. The valley will be anything but flat and will need to be readjusted as you sew the

edge. As you sew, you will also be pulling the edge of the valley to the edge of the hill. You may find a stiletto handy to hold the two pieces together as

you sew. If you don't have a stiletto, you might use the point of a seam ripper. Some people even use a pair of long tweezers. Be sure to remove the pins as you approach them so as not to hit them with your machine needle.

Once the seam is sewn, I clip the seam allowance of the valley every 1/4" or so. This allows the seam to lie flat. I press the seam allowance toward the valley. The hill remains flat. On a rare occasion I will press toward the hill, such as in making the "Sky's the Limit" quilt. When pressing, remember you are doing just that. Press, don't iron!

54-40 or Fight Triangle Unit
The templates provided, or the Tri-Recs ruler, are easy to use as long as you remember one important fact. The triangles from the rectangles (or the "rec" triangles) are directional. This means you will need a half where the diagonal cut is from the upper left corner to the lower right corner of the rectangle and half where the diagonal cut is from the upper right corner to the lower left corner of the rectangle. To achieve this without getting confused, place two strips together, either right sides together or wrong sides together, and cut through both layers at once. This will give you a pair with each cut.

No Template Needleturn Appliqué

For simple appliqué you might like to use a simple technique, requiring different preparation. (I don't recommend this technique for a very complicated block even though there are other appliquérs who wouldn't use any other method no matter how complicated the design.) This time you won't create a template for each appliqué shape, freezer paper or template plastic. Nor will you need a placement overlay.

Begin by tracing the design onto the wrong side of your background fabric. You might be able to get away without using a light table if your background is a light colored fabric. For a light colored background, you may mark with a fine mechanical pencil. You want a thin line, one that does not show through to the right side of your fabric. If using a dark colored background, you will most definitely need to employ a light table and a light colored marking pen. I recommend the Clover White Pen as it won't rub off while you are working.

Cut appliqué fabrics larger than the appliqué shape and place on the right side of the background, over the traced shape, right side up. Using a larger needle, such as a #7 tapestry needle, and a thicker thread, such as a 30-wt cotton thread, baste the fabric to the right side of the background, but stitching from the wrong side. Take small stitches, close together, following the traced line on the background. (9)

Carefully trim the excess appliqué fabric 3/16" outside the basting thread. (10) When you are ready to appliqué, clip the basting thread and remove about an inch or so of the thread.

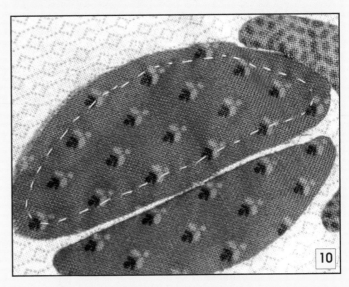

Using your appliqué needle of choice (I use a #11 Straw), turn under the seam allowance, following the holes left by the basting thread. You will match the turned under edge to the holes in the background and stitch. As you need, remove more of the basting thread until you have completed stitching the shape to the background. Turn over the background and you will notice the appliqué stitches are following your traced line or very close to it. (If you miss the line, no one will know the difference!) (11)

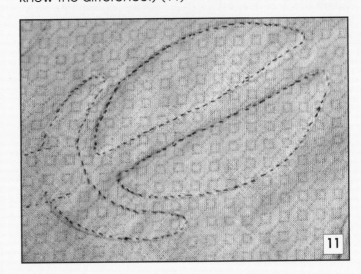

Piecing the Appliqué

Traditionally, appliqué shapes are stitched to the background blocks. I prefer to remove the background from behind the appliqué when possible so I can quilt by hand more successfully. If each of the shapes is stitched one by one, to the background, I cannot remove all the layers of fabric I need to, and the more layers there are to a design, the more fabric to try to quilt through. Therefore, I study each piece and determine which part of each shape is background and which is the appliqué.

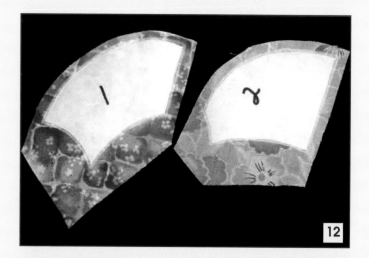

The "background" is any part that will be under an adjacent shape. The "appliqué" is any part that will be stitched; that is, the seam allowance is turned under and the edge stitched to the background block or the adjacent piece. If the part of a shape is the background, I leave about 3/4" or more so I have someplace to pin the next piece while I'm stitching. (12) On the part of the shape that is the appliqué, I cut a 3/16" seam allowance. (13) Please note, 1/4" is too much fabric to turn under and 1/8" is often too narrow, especially if you have a loosely woven fabric for the appliqué, so split the difference. I have been known to use a 1/8" seam allowance if my shape is very small. In that instance, I really try to find a tightly woven fabric, such as cotton Batik, to use. The tighter weave holds together better as I use the needle to turn under the seams.

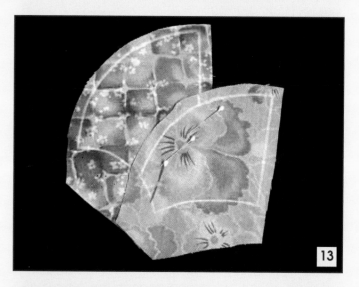

When tracing the templates on the paper side of the freezer paper, I trace the design as a whole. This way, when I cut the templates apart, whatever editing I do with my scissors to a line shared by two shapes, I do equally to the two shapes. I am assured my "puzzle" will always go back together in my stitching.

As I stitch the appliqué, I trim the background out from behind the appliqué. That is, I remove the extra fabric I left by trimming so all the seam allowances are 3/16" on the back of the unit. (14) When all the pieces to a unit are stitched together and the excess is trimmed from behind, I stitch the completed unit to the background block. This allows me to trim the background out from behind the appliqué, removing the excess layer for ease of hand quilting later.

Fusible Appliqué

Fusible appliqué is worked in reverse. The patterns are worked from the wrong side of the fabric, so the patterns need to be reversed in order for the designs to come out correctly. If you were to desire an alphabet, the letters would need to be drawn in reverse. Sometimes the design does not require reversing – a symmetrical design, for instance. You will notice that on Barb Fife's "Sunflower Fields" quilt on page 66, the applique leaves are the reverse of the placement guide. Barb did not reverse the applique shapes before tracing them onto the fusible web. In this case it did not alter the pattern enough to change the appearance.

I suggest using a lightweight paper-backed fusible web product. Check to see if the webbing is still attached to the paper. With age and tight rolling, the web can separate from the paper. A light pressing, from the paper side, onto a non-stick appliqué sheet can re-adhere the web to the paper in a pinch.

Trace each element of the appliqué separately onto the paper side of your fusible web product, leaving about 1/2" between shapes. Follow the directions that came with your fusible product for applying it to the wrong side of your fabric. (Each product on the market has specific and unique directions. Some require steam; some are killed by steam. Read your directions carefully.) Cut each piece out along the traced line. Peel the paper backing off the piece and arrange the pieces on your background fabric and fuse, again following the directions that came with the fusible material. One thing to remember in fused appliqué: no additional seam allowance is added except at the edge that adjoins another shape. Adding a little for underlay insures no gaps will appear.

If you are going to hand quilt your appliquéd quilt, you may consider "windowing" your fusible material. By that I mean, trace the pattern onto the paper side of the fusible, leaving the 1/2" between patterns. Before fusing the material to the wrong side of your fabric, cut out the center of the fusible, leaving only about 1/4" all the way around the edge, creating a window. (This lets the appliqué be

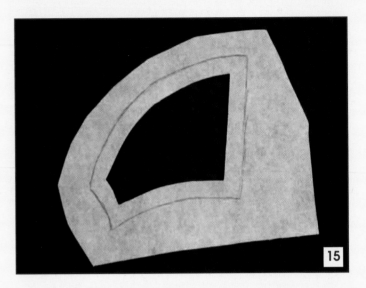

15

adhered to the top while you are stitching but there is no stiff glue to try to hand quilt through.) (15)

After you fuse the web to the back of your fabric, cut the shape out following the line that you traced. Remove the paper backing and arrange the appliqué piece onto the background. Fuse the design in place following the directions that came with your fusible material.

You might consider placing your pattern under the non-stick appliqué sheet. The sheet is translucent enough for you to be able to see the pattern under the pressing sheet. Place your appliqué pieces, with paper backing removed, on the appliqué sheet, arranging them over the pattern. Press the arrangement with your iron just to secure. You can then lift the entire arrangement and place it on the background. Following the directions that came with your product, fuse it to the background.

I use a small "blanket" stitch built into my sewing machine or the "invisible hem" stitch. I use the open toed embroidery foot so that I can see where I am going. I usually use a cotton 50-weight 2-ply thread, matching the color to my appliqué fabrics. I have, however, used a 50-weight silk thread in a contrasting color to create a halo affect. (16) If your machine does not have the blanket stitch, you may use a short, narrow zigzag stitch. By using thread to match, your stitches will not show. (17)

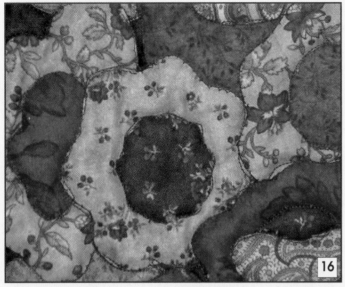

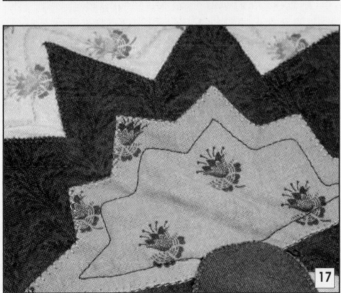

Using a neutral thread or one that blends with the appliqué fabric, sew a straight stitch all around the freezer paper template, taking care to avoid stitching through the paper. Remove the paper and carefully cut away the excess fabric, taking care not to cut the background fabric. (19)

Satin Stitch Appliqué

For visual texture, you might try machine appliqué with a satin stitch. This especially works well with larger, simpler shapes. Begin by tracing the appliqué shape onto the paper side of freezer paper. Cut out the shape and press onto the right side of your appliqué fabric with a dry iron set on wool. Roughly cut out the shape, leaving a half-inch or so extra fabric all around. Place the shape where you want it on the background. (18)

Choose a matching thread or contrasting, decorative thread and set your machine for a satin stitch. Carefully stitch around the appliqué shape, catching the raw edge of the shape and covering the straight stitching. (20)

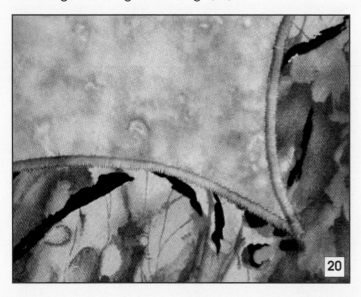

Preparing Your Quilt Top for a Long-arm Quilter

Loading your quilt top and backing onto a long-arm quilting machine is very different from stretching your quilt sandwich on a frame for hand quilting. To begin, your backing needs to be squared and 8" wider and longer than your quilt top. If the backing consists of more than one piece, they need to be the same length. Be sure to remove the selvages before seaming the two pieces together.

Long arm quilters need the backing seams to run parallel to the machine arm to reduce bulk and pull on the back seam. Check with your quilter for his/her preferences. Some quilters load the longest edge onto the machine first so a vertical seam is preferred. Some prefer a horizontal seam. The size of your quilt will contribute to the decision as well.

One who professionally quilts on a domestic sewing machine will have a whole different set of criteria. It is always best to discuss with your quilter every aspect before leaving your quilt top for quilting. This way, there will be no surprises.

Vertical seams are preferred for the back of the quilt, especially if hanging. A single seam in the center may not be ideal. I often put two seams in my backing. I do this by cutting one of the panels for the back into two equal lengths. I place the wider piece in the center and stitch the two narrower pieces to either side. This leaves the center of my quilt seam free.

The straight-of-grain is important if your quilt will be hanging on the wall. Cutting borders and backing across the width of the fabric (the stretchier direction) may cause your quilt to sag over time. For a wall quilt, cutting the length of the fabric, parallel to the selvages, is preferred as it has little or no stretch.

Your long-arm quilter is your partner in making your quilt. Discuss with your quilter what is expected of you in preparing your quilt top for the long-arm quilting machine. Piecing accuracy not only makes your quilt look better, but also makes quilting on the long-arm machine easier. Accuracy counts! Your long-arm quilter will be able to tell you how much larger than the top to make the backing and the batting.

Binding

The loft, or thickness, of the batting you have chosen will determine how wide you will need to cut your strips for the binding. Typically strips for binding are cut anywhere between 2" and 2 1/2" wide. To determine the number of strips that you will need, measure the top and a side, multiply by two (to get the total circumference of your quilt top) and then divide by 40 (the average usable length of a strip cut selvage to selvage, after the selvage is removed). This will give you the number of strips you will need to bind your quilt. Naturally, a partial strip should be counted as a whole strip. So if the number you get is, say, 6.34, then you would cut 7 strips.

To determine the amount of fabric needed for the binding, multiply the number of strips that are needed by 2 1/2" and then round up about 1/8 yard. This gives you enough to straighten the fabric, before you begin cutting the strips, and even to make a mistake. (I always multiply by 2 1/2" even if I'm going to make the strips 2 1/2" wide.) So, say I need 6 strips. That's 15 inches. I'll round up to 1/2 yard (18") and that will give me another strip should I need it. If I had needed exactly 18" I would still have rounded up so that I would have extra "just in case."

Sometimes, if my backing is especially larger than my quilt top, I can cut strips the length of the backing piece. This way I may only need a total of 4 strips and I'll have fewer seams in my binding. Remove the selvages and sew the strips together, end to end, by placing them at a 45-degree angle to each other, right sides together. Stitch on the bias across the tails, not between them. (21) Trim the excess to a 1/4" seam allowance and press the seam open. This will help to eliminate bulk. Press the entire strip in half (the full length) wrong side in. Now you're ready to bind your quilt.

While some quilters trim away the excess batting or backing before adding the binding, I do not. However, I do make sure that the corners are square. Using a 12 1/2" or larger square ruler, I mark the corners square if they have been distorted at all. When sewing the binding to the quilt, I let this line guide me when aligning my binding in the corners, not the edge of the quilt top.

Using a walking or even-feed foot on your sewing machine gives you a better binding. Move your needle to the far right position so that it is 1/4" to 3/8" from the edge of the foot. The edge of the foot will be your sewing guide. At this point I still have not

removed any of the excess batting or backing. I wait to do that after the binding is attached. (There are quilters who use a rotary cutter to remove the excess and square the corners.) I also increase the length of my stitches just a bit since I'm going to be sewing through more thickness than when I piece.

Begin in the center of a side. Leaving a 10" to 12" tail, sew the binding, raw edges to the edge of your quilt top or the marking you made for the square corner. Sew to the corner but not all the way through the corner. Stop the same distance from the corner that your needle is from the edge of the quilt, 1/4" to 3/8". Remove the quilt from under the needle and presser foot and rotate the quilt so that you will be ready to sew the next edge. Before doing so, fold the binding at a 45-degree angle from where you previously stitched. The raw edge of the binding and the raw edge of the quilt top will form a straight line. (22) If not, it's probably because the stitch extends beyond where it should have ended – 1/4" or 3/8" from the end of the seam. If that's the case, then clip that last stitch. This will allow you to pull the binding back farther in order to make that straight line along the raw edge. If it is straight, fold the binding down over the corner, aligning the raw edge with the new side. The fold will align with the previous edge. Begin sewing again from just off the edge to just before the next corner and repeat. (23)

When you get to the final side, stop sewing about 12" to 15" from where you began. At this point there are several ways to finish, some appearing bulkier than others. The method I use isn't really that hard once you get the hang of it and it gives you a smooth join. So let me walk you through this slowly. Once you get it, you'll be delighted with the technique.

Bring the two tails together in the middle of the unsewn space. Fold the tails back on themselves so that there is about a 1/8" gap between the two where the folds meet. Make a small clip though all four layers of the binding fabric right where they meet in the center, perpendicular to the raw edge.

Be sure that your clip is no deeper than about 1/8". You don't want to clip through where you will be sewing your seam. (24)

Now place your quilt on your table so that the edge on which you are working is right in front of you and the rest of the quilt is across the table. Open the left tail. The right side will be toward the quilt top and the wrong side will be showing. Place your left hand, palm up, on the quilt top behind the open binding (the binding is between you and your hand). With your right hand, flip the tail over, toward your hand, so that the wrong side of the binding is now in your hand and the right side is facing up. Angle the end of the tail toward the center of your quilt.

Open the right tail so that the wrong side is facing up and angle it toward the center of the quilt top. Now place the right tail on top of the left tail. Cross them at a 45-degree angle to each other. Match the clips you made so that the correct placement occurs. Place a pin to hold the matched points in place. You will be sewing across the tails, so place your pins perpendicular to the sewing line. (25)

Press the seam open and trim for a 1/4" seam allowance. Fold the binding again as you had in the beginning and press the seam. Align the raw edges to your quilt top and finish sewing the binding to the top between the point where you began and ended. You should notice that the binding is flat and smooth!

Once the binding is attached you are ready to remove the excess batting and backing. I always want to be sure that the batting completely fills my binding. This is why I wait to cut the excess away. To that end I leave about 1/8" extra batting and backing, extending past the raw edge of the binding. (26)

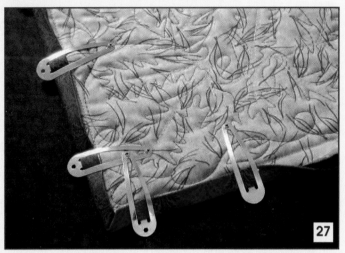

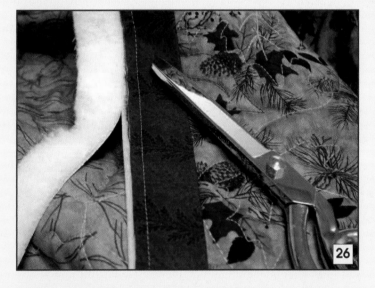

Hand stitch the binding to the back, taking small stitches in the back, being careful not to go all the way through to the front, and then bringing the needle through the fold of the binding. The stitch will be hidden in the fabric. The stitches should be short and close together so that the binding is secure.

At the corners, clip the corner tips off (top, batting and backing, not binding), tuck the fold that is created by the mitered corner in the binding in the opposite direction of the fold on the front side. This will distribute the bulk so that the corner is smoother. If the binding gaps in the corner, stitch the fold. This will make an even neater corner.

To complete the binding, fold the finished edge around the raw edge to the back, just covering the machine stitching. You won't have to pin all of the binding to the back before beginning to stitch, but you will find that securing some as you're working will keep the binding fabric from stretching. Some quilters will use pins, pinning in the direction they stitch so they don't prick their knuckles. My favorite method uses "binding clips" that have, for a previous generation, acted as hair clips! You will find these marvelous tools at your local quilt shop. (27)

SCRAP FRENZY UNDER CONTROL • 67 1/2" x 79 1/2"
Made by Kathy Delaney, Overland Park, Ks. and quilted by Alice Scott, Lenexa, Ks.

Scrap Frenzy Under Control

A quilt made by Nancy Swanwick from Parsons, Kansas, inspired the idea for this pattern. The concept struck me as a terrific way to make a scrappy looking quilt without having a large supply of scraps. In other words, it's perfect for a newer quilter!

It is also an excellent exercise in giving up control. Do you ever have trouble choosing just the right fabric to go in just the right place in your quilt? Do you agonize over fabric choices? This project will give you an opportunity to not worry about matching. In fact, the project takes away from you the control to match!

The size of the quilt is totally up to you. You can make it as large or as small as you like. However, I did try making a 9-block quilt, infant sized, and it didn't turn out so well. All you need to know, fabric wise, is that you need a fat quarter for every block. In other words, if your quilt top has 20 blocks, you need 20 fat quarters. The project on these pages calls for just 20 fat quarters and 1/2 yard for binding. Add the backing fabric and that's it! The chart below will help you decide how much fabric for the size you wish to make.

Layout	Size	# of blocks/ fat quarters
4 blocks / 5 rows	48" x 60"	20
5 blocks / 5 rows	60" x 60"	25
9 blocks / 10 rows	108" x 120"	90

Choose fat quarters that you like together. Feel free to throw in a couple you don't think "match." These zingers are often what make the quilt work. Choosing the fabric is the only place you have any control over your fabric choices once you begin sewing. So, choose lights, mediums and darks, large-scale prints, medium-scale prints and small-scale prints. And don't forget geometrics and plaids!

Fabric (The project on these pages is for the first layout listed on the chart)

20 fat quarters (18" x 22" rectangle) – this is the only place you have any control over your fabric choices. Choose fabrics that please you as they are put together. Choose lights, mediums, and darks, large scale prints, medium scale, and small scale. And don't forget to choose geometrics and plaids. Also, don't think all watercolor or hand dyed fabrics or those wonderful Batik fabrics will work. Once they are cut into pieces you may find they are so close in appearance that they get lost or appear as a solid. Don't be afraid to choose one or two "uglies!"

1/2 yard for border #1

1 7/8 yards for border #2

5/8 yard for binding

4 yards for backing

You will need to be somewhat organized when you cut your fabrics. Each element that you cut from each of the fat quarters will need to be put into one of (9) zip-closed bags. Label them 1 – 9 and have them close by as you cut. You will also need some pins to make sure your pieces stay together until you need them for block construction. When I pinned the pieces, I was careful to pin in the direction of the grain, not through the bias, so as to avoid distorting the pieces.

Cutting

You can stack and cut 4 or 5 fat quarters at a time. I recommend you begin with a new or newly sharpened blade in your rotary cutter. You will be cutting 9 elements as listed below. As you cut the element, place it in the marked receptacles. (i.e. bag #1, bag #2, bag #3 and so on to bag #9.) Each pin will hold element sets of one fabric at a time only.

I followed the diagram below for my cutting sequence.

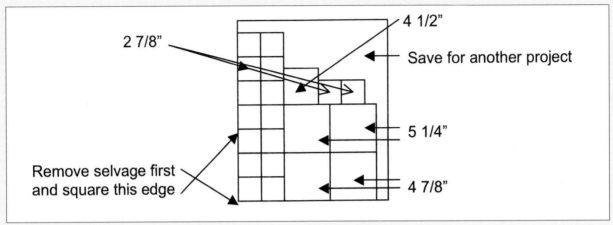

Cutting the Fat Quarters

#1: Cut (4) 2 7/8" squares. Cut diagonally once for (8) 1/2-square triangles. Pin sets together and place in bag #1.

#2: Cut (2) 2 7/8" squares. Cut diagonally once for (4) 1/2-square triangles. Pin sets together and place in bag #2.

#3: Cut (2) 2 7/8" squares. Cut diagonally once for (4) 1/2-square triangles. Pin sets together and place in bag #3.

#4: Cut (4) 2 7/8" squares. Cut diagonally once for (8) 1/2-square triangles. Pin sets together and place in bag #8.

#5: Cut (4) 2 7/8" squares. Cut diagonally once for (8) 1/2-square triangles. Pin sets together and place in bag #5.

#6: Cut (2) 4 7/8" squares. Cut diagonally once for (4) 1/2-square triangles. Pin sets together and place in bag #6.

(You will have five sets of 2 7/8; 1/2-square triangles from each fat quarter and one set of 4 7/8" 1/2-square triangles.)

#7: Cut (1) 5 1/4" square. Cut diagonally twice for (4) 1/4-square triangles. Pin sets together and place in bag #7.

#8: Cut (1) 5 1/4" square. Cut diagonally twice for (4) additional 1/4-square triangles. Pin sets together and place in bag #8.

(You will have two sets of 1/4-square triangles from each fat quarter.)

#9: Cut (1) 4 1/2" square and place in bag #9.

Constructing the Block

The 12" finished block is a variation on the traditional Corn and Beans, a 9-Patch block, consisting of (4) units A, (4) units B and (1) 4 1/2" square from bag #9. Each of the units will use elements from the bags. You have just 2 rules in pulling the fabric pieces for these blocks:

1. You may not look. Whatever you pick is what you use, even if it is the same fabric as another you've already picked.

2. The only time you may choose something different is if you will end up with two patches next to each other out of the same fabric.

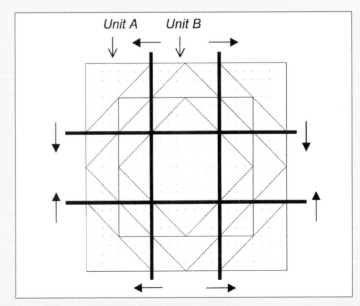

The block diagram on the bottom of pg. 16 shows you how the units combine to make the block. Notice the corner units are all the same and the side units are all the same. The dark arrows refer to the pressing direction of the seam allowances.

The numbers in the photos of the units correspond to the bags. Pull from the bags as indicated and construct four each of the units A and B.

Pressing the blocks will be very important. Follow the pressing instructions carefully. Notice the direction in which the seam allowance is to be pressed. Even though the direction appears wrong to you as you press the seams of each unit (based on past quilt making experience), it will pay off as you construct the blocks and ultimately, the quilt top. And as you press the units, DO NOT touch the iron to the bias edges.

Unit A – make (4) the same

Begin by sewing a #2 to a #3. Press the seam allowance toward #2. Sew a #5 to each side of the #3 and press the seam allowances toward #3. Sew a #6 to the triangle unit and press the seam allowance toward #6. Trim all of the little triangles (the "dog ears" or "bunny ears") to straighten the edges. Completed unit will measure 4 1/2" square. Make sure you are stitching with an accurate 1/4" seam allowance. This means the stitching and the thread are included in the 1/4".

Unit A – make (4) the same

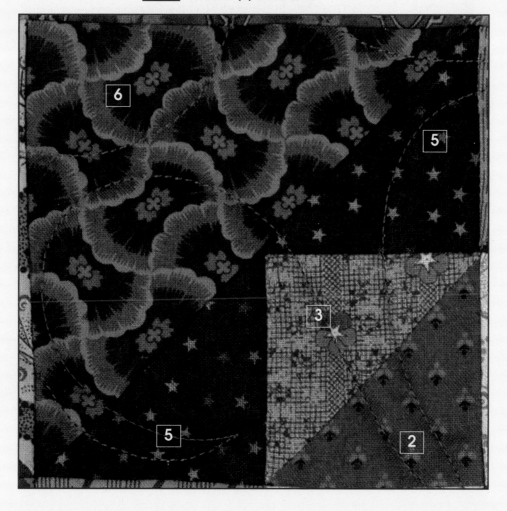

Unit B – make (4) the same

Sew the small triangles to the short sides of the large triangles, being sure to pair the fabrics according to the photo for two flying geese units. Press the seam allowances toward the smaller triangles. Sew the two flying geese units as the diagram shows, making sure of fabric placement. Press the seam allowances toward #8. Trim all of the little triangles (the "dog ears" or "bunny ears") to straighten the edges.

Following the diagram of the block on page 16, arrange the Units A and the Units B around the center square. Sew the units into rows and the rows into a block.

Repeat, sewing one block at a time until all the blocks are complete.

Unit B – make (4) the same

Putting It All Together
Once you have constructed all 20 blocks, arrange them as it pleases you, into 5 rows of 4 blocks each.

I include a border on this quilt. However, I think the binding would serve to frame the quilt if you prefer to make a smaller quilt or make more blocks for a much larger quilt.

Border #1
Cut (6) 2" strips, selvage to selvage. Cut (2) of the strips in half for about a 22" strip. Sew the 22" strips to the end of each of the full strips. Measure through the vertical center of the quilt top and cut (2) pieced strips to that length. Sew to the right and left sides of the quilt top. Press the seam allowances toward the strips.

Measure the horizontal center of the quilt top. Cut the remaining (2) pieced strips to that length. Sew to the top and bottom of your quilt top. Press the seam allowances toward the strips.

Border #2
Remove the selvages from the border fabric and cut (4) 8 1/2" wide strips from the length of the fabric. Measure through the vertical center of the quilt top and cut (2) strips to that length. Measure through the horizontal center of the quilt top and cut (2) strips that length.

Sew the first (2) strips to the right and left sides of the quilt top. Press the seam allowances toward the strips.

From what you have left of your fat quarters, cut (8) 4 7/8" squares, (2) from each of (4) prints. Cut each square diagonally for (2) 1/2-square triangles. From (4) other prints cut (4) 6 1/8" squares.

To each of the squares, sew (4) matching triangles. Press the seam allowances toward the triangles. Repeat for a total of (4) 8 1/2" square-in-a-square units. Sew the units to the ends of the remaining (2) border strips, pressing the seam allowances toward the border strips.

Sew the pieced border strips to the top and bottom of your quilt top. Press the seam allowances toward the strips.

Quilting
An over-all pattern would certainly be a good addition to this quilt design. Because of all the sharp angles in the blocks, you might consider a design with softer curves to contrast.

Binding
Cut (8) strips from your binding fabric. Depending on the loft of your batting and the width of your seam allowance when you sew the binding to your quilt top, your strips may be anywhere from 2 1/8" wide to 2 1/2" wide. I have given you enough fabric in the amount listed for a 2 1/2" wide binding.

Sew the strips together with a bias seam, end-to-end (following the instructions for binding beginning on page 10), and press the seam allowances open to reduce bulk. Fold the strip in half, lengthwise, wrong side in, and press. Sew the binding to your quilt top with a 1/4" seam, fold the finished edge to the back and stitch to the back, mitering the corners.

A Note
I taught this quilt to a group of quilters. At the end of the class they all exhibited the blocks they had completed. All the fabric choices were totally different, yet when we put all the blocks together as if to arrange a quilt top, the resulting design looked fabulous! I think this served to prove you don't necessarily have to begin with coordinating fat quarters and this quilt could easily be made by a group of quilters as a presentation quilt for a deserving friend.

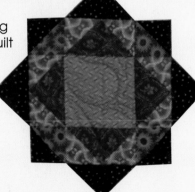

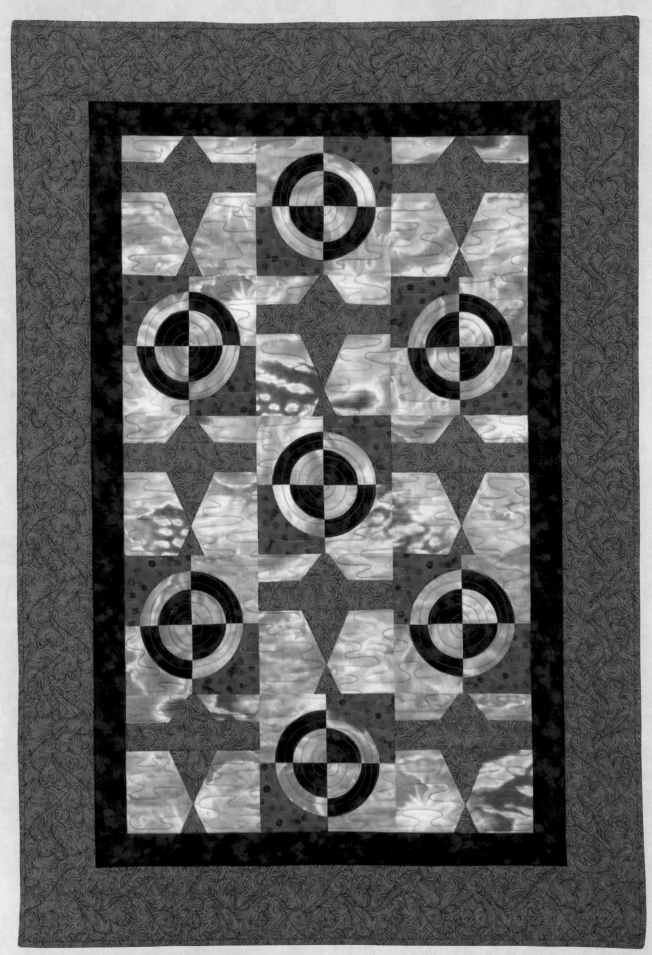

SKY'S THE LIMIT CRIB QUILT • 35 1/2" x 51 1/2"
Made by Natalie Hutchison, Olathe, Ks. and quilted by Freda Smith, Kansas City, Ks.

Fabric

1 5/8 yards light blue for sky in airplane blocks and propeller blocks
3/4 yard royal blue for propeller blocks
3/4 yard navy blue for propeller blocks
1 3/4 yards red for airplane blocks, border and binding
1/3 yard navy for inner border
1 1/2 yards for backing

Additional tools

Add-a-Quarter Template Guide/Ruler
28 mm rotary cutter
Small rotary cutting mat

Airplane Blocks (make 8)

Cutting instructions (All cuts are from the width of the fabric unless otherwise noted)

From the sky blue:
Cut (3) 3" strips. Sub-cut (16) 3" x 5 1/2" rectangles. (Pieces A-2 and A-3)
Cut (2) 6" strips. Sub-cut (16) 6" x 5" rectangles. (Pieces C-1 and B-1)

From the red:
Cut (1) 3" strip. Sub-cut (8) 3" x 5" rectangles. (Piece A-1)
Cut (2) 3" strips. Sub-cut (8) 3" x 9 1/2" rectangles. (Piece A-4)
Cut (1) 3 1/2" strip. Sub-cut (8) 3 1/2" squares. (Piece B-2)
Cut (1) 5" strip. Sub-cut (8) 5" x 4 1/2" rectangles. (Piece C-2)

Constructing the blocks

Following the instructions for Freezer Paper Foundation Piecing on page 3, create (7) airplane blocks (each block is made from 3 segments). The numbers of the patterns correspond to the stitching sequence.

Sewing fabric to the paper segment patterns

Place red fabric for A-1 behind the pattern, wrong side of fabric to shiny side of paper, making sure to center the fabric so there is ample seam allowance all around. Press with a dry iron set on wool. (I set the pattern onto the fabric, wrong side up, and then press. I can see through the paper enough for place-ment, and the iron then only touches the paper side of the freezer paper – no wax on my iron.) Fold the pattern back on the line between A-1 and A-2. Trim a 1/4" seam allowance in the excess fabric using the Add-a-Quarter ruler and the 28 mm rotary cutter. (The 18 mm rotary cutter will not work with the Add-a-Quarter ruler and the 45 or 60 mm rotary cutter is too large, therefore dangerous to use in this technique.)

Align blue fabric for A-2 to the just-cut edge — aligning the fabric with the patch you'll be covering on the paper, not the fabric you've already attached. (Sometimes they will match but often they don't, so don't rely on the previous patch; sew right next to the folded paper. Press open to the freezer paper.

Fold the pattern back on the line between A-3 and the sewn unit. Trim a 1/4" seam allowance as before.

Align blue fabric for A-3 to the just cut edge. Sew right next to the folded paper. You might find trimming the corner (set the fabric next to the pattern and turn the corner back so the fold matches the line. Finger press and then cut on the crease) to make alignment a little easier. Press open to the freezer paper.

Fold the pattern back on the line between #4 and the sewn unit. Trim a 1/4" seam allowance.

Align red fabric for A-4 to the just-cut edge and sew next to the folded paper. Press open to the freezer paper.

Continue to piece Units B and C in the same sequence.

When all patches are sewn and pressed to the freezer paper unit patterns, trim around the units, adding a 1/4" seam allowance, using a rotary cutter and rotary cutting ruler. Be sure to use the same ruler to trim each of the units and be as accurate as possible when measuring your 1/4" seam allowance. Peel the paper pattern from the back of the block. The freezer paper pattern may be reused. Sew the segments together to form the block. With the seam allowances pressed toward the red in units B and C, you will find the intersection easy to match. If you press the new seam in the same direction as the original seams, you will have a flat intersection. (1)

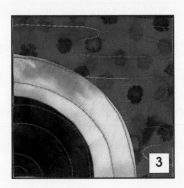

Propeller blocks (make 7)

Each of the pieces that make this block has at least one bias edge. It will be very easy to stretch the pieces, especially the Bs, and cause the block to distort. I recommend you heavily starch the fabrics before cutting your shapes. The starch will help support the fabric, making handling the pieces easier.

Cutting instructions

Using the templates provided, cut shapes as listed below:

    Cut (14) As from the sky blue fabric.
    Cut (14) As from the royal blue fabric.
    Cut (14) Bs from the sky blue fabric.
    Cut (14) Bs from the navy blue fabric.
    Cut (14) Cs from the sky blue fabric.
    Cut (14) Cs from the navy blue fabric.

Constructing the blocks

Following the instructions for curved piecing beginning on pg. 4, make the arc units. Each block is made from (2) units in colorway A (2) and (2) units in colorway B (3). Make a total of (14) of each of the units.

Colorway A

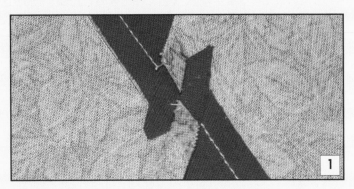

Colorway B

Sew a shape B to a shape C. Cut the seam allowance on the sewn shape B, clipping about every 1/4". Press the seam allowance toward shape B very carefully, avoiding touching the bias edge with the iron.

Sew a shape A to the B/C piece. Press the seam allowance toward the shape B. This will give the arc a little dimension. You will not need to clip the seam allowance on this seam.

When pressing, take care to avoid distorting the block. Each of the units should measure 4 1/2" square. Each propeller block uses (2) A units and (2) B units, sewn into a 4-patch block.

Natalie tells me she used a pressing cloth when giving the blocks a final press. Her thinking was this would prevent the starch from scorching and it would prevent a shine on the seam edges.

Constructing the Quilt Top

Alternating the Airplane blocks and the Propeller blocks, sew (5) rows of (3) blocks each. The odd numbered rows will begin and end with an Airplane block. The even numbered blocks will begin and end with a Propeller block.

Inner border

Cut (4) 2 1/4" wide strips from the navy blue fabric.

Measure through the vertical center of your quilt top. Trim (2) of the 2 1/4" strips to that measurement and sew to the sides of your quilt top. Press the seam allowances toward the strips.

Measure through the horizontal center of your quilt top. Trim the (2) remaining strips to that measurement. Sew to the top and bottom of your quilt top. Press the seam allowances toward the strips.

Outer border

Cut (5) 4 1/2" strips from the red fabric. Cut one of the strips into (2) equal lengths, 4 1/2" wide. Sew these pieces to the ends of (2) of the strips, making them about 62" x 4 1/2" long.

Measure through the vertical center of the quilt top. Trim the pieced strips to that measurement and sew to the sides of your quilt top. Press the seam allowances toward the strips.

Measure through the horizontal center of the quilt top. Trim the remaining (2) strips to that measurement and sew to the top and bottom of your quilt top. Press the seam allowances toward the strips.

Quilting

Freda Smith quilted Natalie's quilt. She quilted spirals in the propellers, making them look as if they are spinning. She outlined the planes and quilted wavy "air" everywhere else. The outer border has a feathery design that reminds me of birds' wings.

Binding

The batting you use and the desired width of the finished binding determine the width of the strips for double fold binding. The amount of fabric listed in the requirements list is enough for a 2 1/2" wide strip. I often use cotton batting that is 80% cotton and 20% polyester. This batting has a little bit of loft for a more sculpted look to my finished quilts. I cut my strips 2 1/8" wide. Sewing the binding on with a 1/4" seam allowance, trimming the batting and backing just a bit wider than the seam allowance gives me about a 3/8" finished binding.

Cut (5) strips between 2 1/8" and 2 1/2" wide, depending on your batting choice and desired binding width. Sew the strips together, end-to-end, sewing 45-degree seams. Press the seams open and trim to a 1/4" seam allowance.

Fold the strip in half the full length, wrong side in. Following the binding directions beginning on page 10, apply the binding to the right side of the quilt sandwich. Pull the folded edge of the strip to the back and hand stitch to the back of the quilt sandwich, taking care to cover the machine stitching.

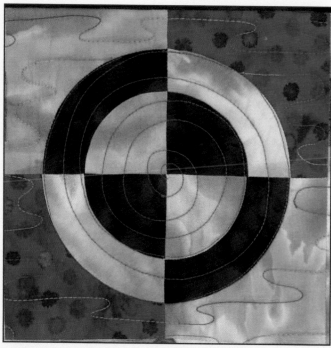

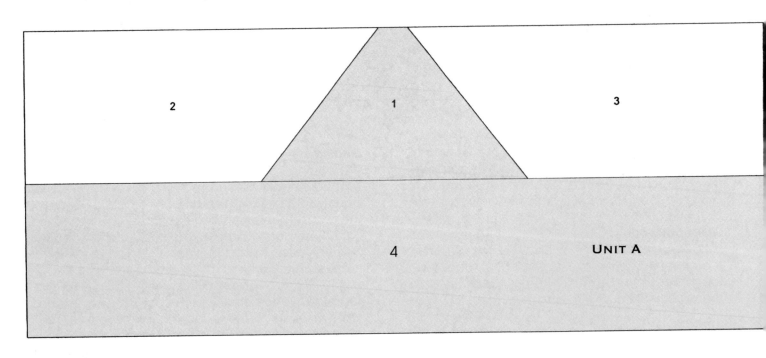

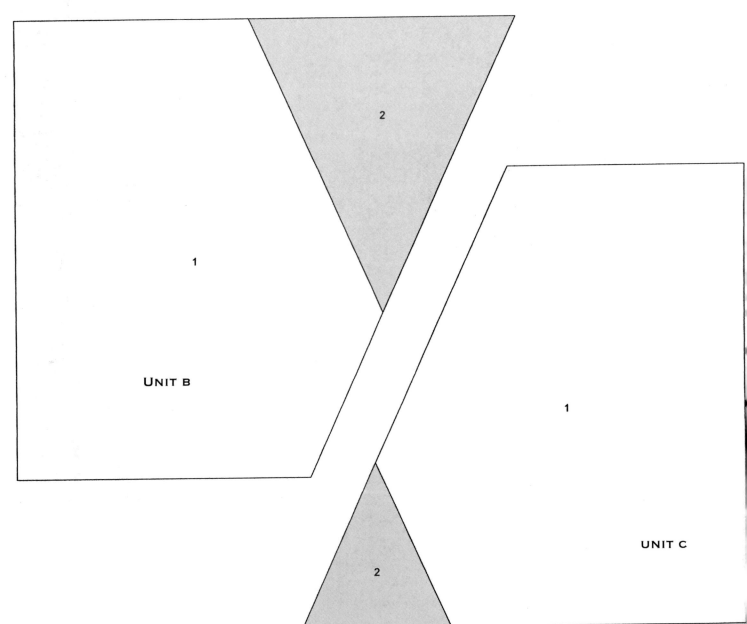

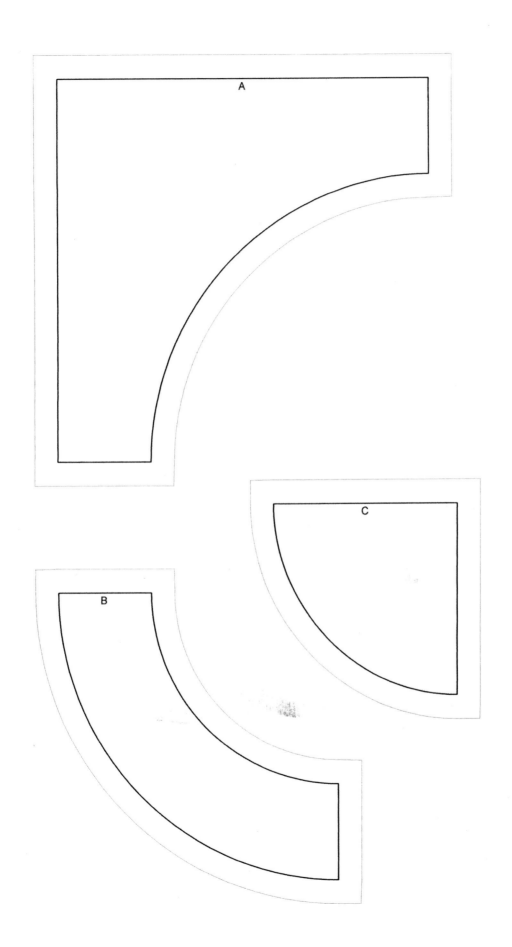

A

C

B

STARLIGHT STARBRIGHT • *70" x 70"*
Made by Jeanne Poore, Overland Park, Ks. and
machine quilted by Freda Smith, Kansas City, Ks.

Fabric (Before you choose your fabrics, please read the section about bindings in this pattern. You have some choices to make!)

    #1 – black – 2 yards
    #2 – yellow – 2 1/3 yards
    #3 – blue – 2 1/2 yards
    #4 – orange – 1/2 yard for blocks and
        5/8 yard for binding
    #5 – gray – 3/8 yard
    Backing – 4 1/2 yards

Cutting Instructions

I have tried to find a generic ruler that would allow me to cut these triangle units but have, so far, been unsuccessful. I suggest using the Tri-Recs Tools, designed by Darlene Zimmerman and Joy Hoffman for EZ Quilting. The tools consist of two rulers, one for the "tri" triangle and one for the "rec" triangle. I include templates for the triangle units for those of you who prefer.

Fabric #1 – black:
    Cut (10) 5 1/2" strips. Sub-cut (200)
        rec triangles.
    Cut (3) 4" strips. Sub-cut (25) 4" squares.

Fabric #2 – yellow:
    Cut (5) 5 1/2" strips. Sub-cut (60) tri triangles.
    Cut (3) 4 3/4" strips. Sub-cut (24) 4 3/4"
        squares. Cut each square diagonally in
        both directions for (96) 1/4-square triangles.
    Cut (4) 4 3/8" strips. Sub-cut (32) 4 3/8" squares.
    Cut each square diagonally once for (64)
        1/2-square triangles.
    Cut (4) 3 3/8" strips. Sub-cut (36) 3 3/8" squares.
    Cut (6) of the squares diagonally once for (12)
        small 1/2-square triangles.

Fabric #3 – blue:
    Cut (2) 8 1/4" strips. Cut (7) 8 1/4" squares. Cut
        each square diagonally in both directions for
        (28) 1/4-square triangles.
    Cut (4) 5 1/2" strips. Sub-cut (40) tri triangles.
    Cut (2) 4 3/4" strips. Sub-cut (16) 4 3/4" squares.
    Cut each square diagonally in both directions
        for (64) 1/4-square triangles.

Cut (3) 4 3/8" strips. Sub-cut (18) 4 3/8" squares.
Cut each of the squares diagonally for (36)
    1/2-square triangles.
Cut (4) 3 3/8" strips. Sub-cut (42) 3 3/8" squares.
Cut (26) of the squares diagonally once for
    (52) 1/2-square triangles. Set aside the
    remaining (16) squares.

Fabric #4 – orange:
    Cut (3) 3 3/8" strips. Sub-cut (34) 3 3/8" squares.
    Cut (18) of the squares diagonally once for
        (36) 1/2-square triangles. Set aside the
        remaining (16) squares.

Fabric #5 – gray:
    Cut (3) 3 3/8" strip. Sub-cut (24) 3 3/8" squares.

The Blocks: 14" finished

Sew (2) black rec triangles to each of the (60) yellow tri triangles for (60) "tri-recs" triangles units.

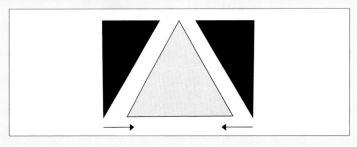

Sew (2) black rec triangles to each of (40) blue tri triangles for (40) tri-recs triangle units.

Pair each of the gray 3 3/8" squares with yellow 3 3/8" squares, right sides together. Mark a line diagonally on the wrong side of the yellow squares and sew 1/4" on either side of the line. Cut on the line and press open, pressing the seam allowance toward the gray. You should have (48) yellow and gray 1/2-square triangle units.

Pair the (16) 3 3/8" orange squares with the (16) blue squares, right sides together. Mark a line diagonally on the wrong side of the orange squares and sew 1/4" on either side of the line. Cut on the line and press open, pressing the seam allowance toward the blue. You should have (32) orange and blue 1/2-square triangle units.

Sew an orange 1/2-square triangle to opposite sides of each of the 4" black squares. Press the seam allowance toward the triangles. You can easily align the triangle to the square. Fold the triangle in half along the long edge and finger press the crease. Fold the square in half and match the center crease to the crease you made in the center of the triangle.

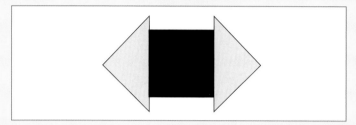

Sew an orange 1/2-square triangle to the top and bottom of the squares. Press the seam allowance toward the triangles. You will have (9) square-in-a-square units.

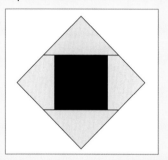 

Sew (4) blue 1/2-square triangles to each of (4) 4" black squares for (4) blue and black square-in-a-square units, in the same manner as the orange.

Sew (3) blue and (1) yellow 1/2-square triangles to (12) 4" black squares for (12) blue, yellow and black square-in-a-square units.

Block #1 – Make (9) blocks
For each of the 9 blocks you will need:

(4) yellow tri-recs triangle units
(4) yellow and gray 1/2-square triangle units
(4) large yellow 1/2-square triangles
(8) yellow 1/4-square triangles
(1) orange and black square-in-a-square unit.

Sew a yellow 1/4-square triangle to each of the gray sides of the 1/2-square triangle units. Press the seam allowances toward the 1/4-square triangles. Think of this as a "birds in the air" unit.

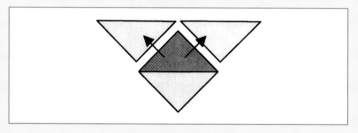

Sew (2) of the birds in the air units to either side of (2) of the tri-recs triangle units. Refer to the block photograph above for placement.

Referring to the block photo, sew a large yellow 1/2-square triangle to the yellow end of each of the yellow tri-recs triangle units.
Sew the base of a yellow tri-recs triangle unit to opposite sides of the square-in-a-square unit.

You should have (3) rows now to complete your block as shown.

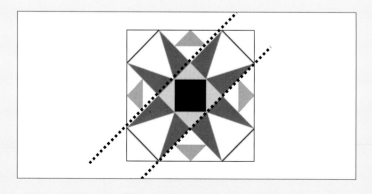

Block #2 – Make (12) blocks
For each of the 12 blocks you will need:

(2) blue tri-recs triangle units
(2) yellow tri-recs triangle units
(1) large blue 1/4-square triangle
(2) orange and blue 1/2-square triangle units
(1) yellow and gray 1/2-square triangle units
(2) large blue 1/2-square triangles
(2) large yellow 1/2-square triangles
(4) small blue 1/4-square triangles
(2) yellow 1/4-squre triangles
(3) small blue 1/2-square triangles
(1) small yellow 1/2-square triangle
(1) black square

The blocks are constructed the same way as block #1. However, the large blue 1/4-square triangle in block #2 replaces one of the birds in the air units in block #1. Refer to the block photo above for unit and color placement.

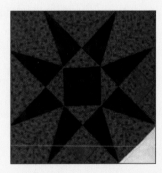

Block #3 – Make (4) blocks
For each of the 4 blocks you will need:

(4) blue tri-recs triangle units
(2) large blue 1/4-square triangles
(2) orange and blue 1/2-square triangle units
(4) small blue 1/4-square triangles
(3) large blue 1/2-square triangles
(4) small blue 1/2-square triangles
(1) large yellow 1/2-square triangle
(1) black square

The blocks are constructed the same way as block #1. However, the (2) large blue 1/4-square triangles in block #3 replace (2) of the birds in the air units in block #1. Refer to the block photo for unit and color placement.

Putting it All Together
Arrange the blocks in 5 rows of 5 blocks each. Arrange the blocks as shown in the photo of the quilt.

Quilting
Freda Smith used her long-arm quilting machine to finish Jeanne's quilt. Freda outline stitched "in the ditch" around each of the triangles and black star points. In the background she created a feather design to fill each space.

A feather or cable design, superimposed over the blue border and circular patterns within the yellow circles might be interesting, too.

Binding
When I designed this quilt I thought the orange would make a perfect binding. But when Jeanne was making the sample, she just could not get her mind around the orange! So she substituted black, not having enough of the

blue and not being able to find any more of the same fabric. I still think an orange frame would have been dynamite (see page 90), so the fabric requirement list gives the 1/2 yard of orange for the binding. But if you want to use something else, just buy 5/8 yard of your choice.

From the remaining orange fabric, cut enough 2" to 2 1/2" strips (depending on the batting you use and how wide you like your bindings) that, when sewn together end to end (following the binding instructions begining on page 10), will equal the outside measurement of your quilt top, about 280 inches. Depending on the width of the fabric, you may need (7) or (8) strips.

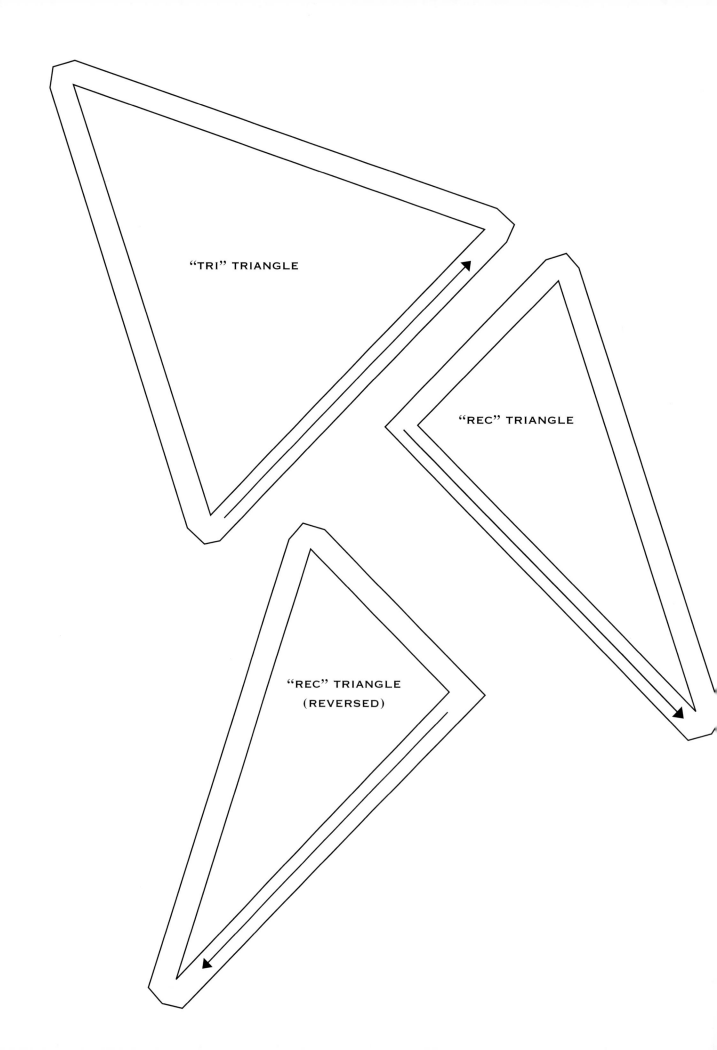

"TRI" TRIANGLE

"REC" TRIANGLE

"REC" TRIANGLE
(REVERSED)

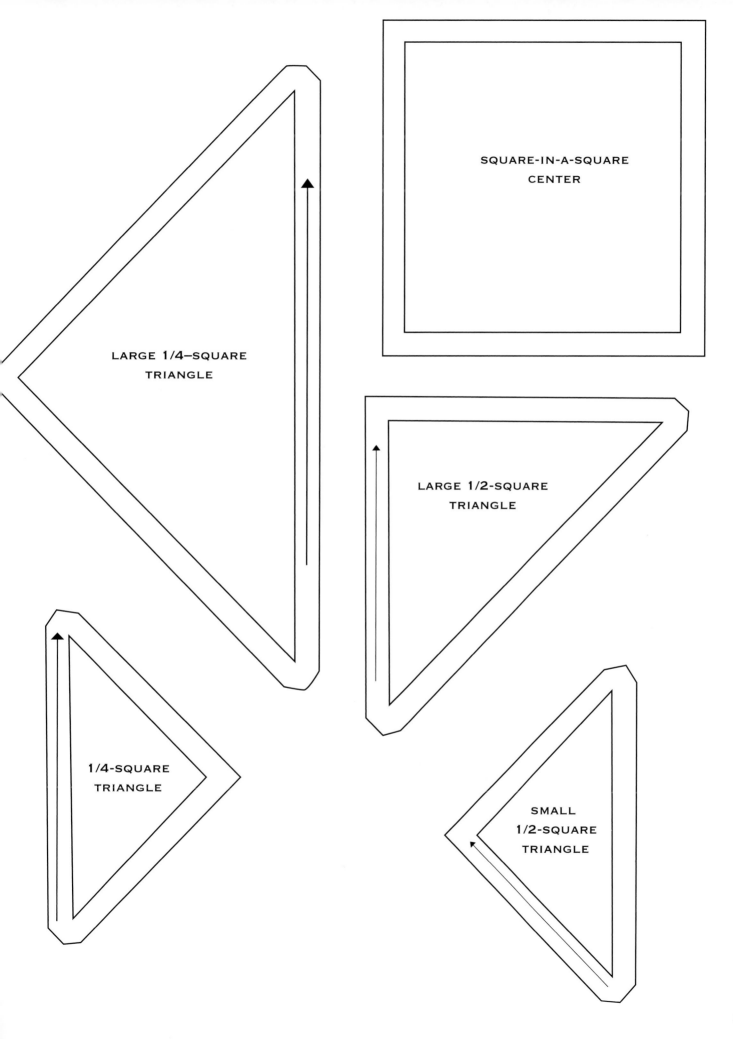

LARGE 1/4—SQUARE
TRIANGLE

SQUARE-IN-A-SQUARE
CENTER

LARGE 1/2-SQUARE
TRIANGLE

1/4-SQUARE
TRIANGLE

SMALL
1/2-SQUARE
TRIANGLE

54-40 OR FLIGHT • 49 1/2" square
Made by Linda Mooney, Shawnee, Ks.

This quilt consists of just one block, the traditional "54-40 or Fight." What makes this quilt different from the traditional is the fabric placement. The design flows outside the block. It is each block's coloring that makes up the whole design.

Fabric

Black for background and border #2 – 3 yards

Fabric #1 – kelly green – 1/4 yard

#2 – red – 1/4 yard for blocks and 1/3 yard for border #1

#3 – purple – 1/4 yard

#4 – yellow – 1/3 yard

#5 – blue – 1/3 yard

#6 – lime – 1/4 yard

#7 – teal – 1/8 yard

#8 – lavender – 1/8 yard

#9 – orange – 1/8 yard

#10 – hot pink – 1/8 yard

Backing – 1 3/4 yard if pieced to fit

Cutting Instuctions

I have tried to find a generic ruler that would allow me to cut these triangle units but have, so far, been unsuccessful. I suggest using the Tri-Recs Tools, designed by Darlene Zimmerman and Joy Hoffman for EZ Quilting. The tools include two rulers, one for the" tri" triangle and one for the "rec" triangle. I include templates for the triangle units for those of you who prefer.

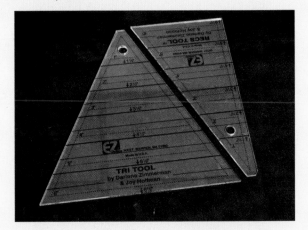

Black: Cut (5) 4 1/2" strips. Sub-cut (16) 4 1/2" squares and (64) rec triangles. Cut (7) 2 1/2" strips. (These are for all the blocks.)

Fabric #1 – kelly green:
Cut (1) 4 1/2" strip. Sub-cut (6) tri triangles.
Sew (2) black rec triangles to each of the tri triangles for (6) 4 1/2" square units.
(For blocks # 4, 7 and 8.)

Fabric #2 – red:
Cut (1) 4 1/2" strip. Sub-cut (8) tri triangles.
Sew (2) black rec triangles to each of the tri triangles for (8) 4 1/2" square units.
Cut (4) 2 1/2" strips and set aside for border #1.
(For blocks #2, 4, 5, 6 and 8)

Fabric #3 – purple:
Cut (1) 4 1/2" strip. Sub-cut (6) tri triangles.
Sew (2) black rec triangles to each of the tri triangles for (6) 4 1/2" square units.
(For blocks #6, 8 and 9.)

Fabric #4 – yellow:
Cut (1) 4 1/2" strip. Sub-cut (6) tri triangles.
Sew (2) black rec triangles to each of the tri triangles for (6) 4 1/2" square units.
Cut (1) 2 1/2" strip. Sew to a 2 1/2" black strip, pressing the seam allowance toward the black.
Sub-cut (12) 2 1/2" segments and sew them into (6) 4-patch units.
(For blocks #1, 2, 6 and 8.)

Fabric #5 – blue:
Cut (1) 4 1/2" strip. Sub-cut (6) tri triangles.
Sew (2) black rec triangles to each of the tri triangles for (6) 4 1/2" square units.
Cut (1) 2 1/2" x 12" strip. Sew to a 2 1/2" x 12" black strip, pressing seam allowance toward the black.
Sub-cut (4) 2 1/2" segments and sew them into (2) 4-patch units.
Cut (2) 2 1/2" squares.
(For blocks # 1, 2, 4, 6 and 8.)

Fabric #6 – lime:
Cut (1) 2 1/2" strip. Sew to a 2 1/2" black strip, pressing the seam allowance toward the black.
Sub-cut (14) 2 1/2" segments and sew them into (7) 4-patch units.
Cut (8) 2 1/2" squares.
(For blocks # 1, 5 and 9.)

Fabric #7 – teal:
    Cut (1) 2 1/2" strip. Sew to a 2 1/2" black strip, pressing the seam allowance toward the black. Sub-cut (10) 2 1/2" segments and sew them into (5) 4-patch units.
    Cut (4) 2 1/2" squares.
    (For blocks #2 and 4.)

Fabric #8 – lavender:
    Cut (1) 2 1/2" strip. Sew to a 2 1/2" black strip, pressing the seam allowance toward the black. Sub-cut (6) 2 1/2" segments and sew them into (3) 4-patch units.
    (For block #7.)

Fabric #9 – orange:
    Cut (1) 2 1/2" x 22" strip. Sew to a 2 1/2" x 22" black strip, pressing the seam allowance toward the black. Sub-cut (8) 2 1/2" segments and sew them into (4) 4-patch units.
    Cut (4) 2 1/2" squares.
    (For blocks #2 and 6.)

Fabric #10 – hot pink:
    Cut (1) 2 1/2" strip. Sew to a 2 1/2" black strip, pressing the seam allowance toward the black. Sub-cut (4) 2 1/2" segments and sew them into (2) 4-patch units.
    Cut (2) 2 1/2" squares.
    (For block #9.)

The Blocks: 12" finished

You will be making 9 blocks, each with a different combination of fabrics. However, each of the blocks will be constructed in the same way. In essence, these blocks are 9-patch blocks.

Block #1

You will need (4) triangle units from fabric (2) 4-patch units from fabric #5 and (2) 4-patch units from fabric #6. Make (1) 4-patch unit using (2) 2 1/2" squares from fabric #5 and (2) 2 1/2" squares from fabric #6. Arrange the units according to the photo of block #1.

Block #2

You will need (1) triangle unit each from fabrics #2, #4 and #5. You will need (2) 4-patch units from fabric #7 and (2) 4-patch units from fabric #9. Make (1) 4-patch unit using (2) 2 1/2" squares from fabric #7 and (2) 2 1/2" squares from fabric #9. You will also need (1) 4 1/2" square from black. Arrange the units according to the photo of block #2.

Block #3

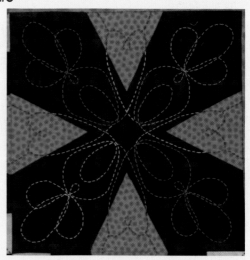

You will need (4) triangle units from fabric #5 and (5) 4 1/2" black squares. Arrange the units according to the photo of block #3.

Block #4

You will need (1) triangle unit each from fabrics #1, #2 and #4. You will need (3) 4-patch units from fabric #7 and (3) 4 1/2" black squares. Arrange the units according to the photo of block #4.

Block #5

You will need (4) triangle units from fabric #2, (2) 4 1/2" black squares and (3) 4-patch units from fabric #6. Arrange the units according to the photo of block #5.

Block #6

You will need (1) triangle unit each from fabrics #2, #3, and #5, (2) 4-patch units from fabric #4 and the black and (2) 4-patch units from fabric #9 and the black. Make (1) 4-patch unit using (2) 2 1/2" squares from fabric #4 and (2) 2 1/2" squares from fabric #9. You will also need (1) 4 1/2" black square. Arrange the units according to the photo of block #6.

Block #7

You will need (4) triangle units from fabric #1, (2) 4 1/2" black squares and (3) 4-patch units from fabric #8. Arrange the units according to the photo of block #7.

Block #8

You will need (1) triangle unit each from fabrics #1, #2 and #3. You will need (3) 4 1/2" black squares and (3) 4-patch units from fabric #4. Arrange the units according to the photo of block #8.

Block #9

You will need (4) triangle units from fabric #3, (2) 4-patch units from fabric #6 and (2) 4-patch units from fabric #10. Make (1) 4-patch unit using (2) 2 1/2" squares from fabric #6 and (2) 2 1/2" squares from fabric #10. Arrange the units according to the photo of Block #9.

Putting it All Together

Arrange the blocks in order as shown in the picture of the quilt and sew into rows and sew the rows into the quilt top.

Measure through the vertical center of your quilt top. Trim two of the 2 1/2" strips you set aside for border #1 to that length and sew to the sides of your quilt top.

Measure through the horizontal center of your quilt top. Trim the remaining 2 1/2" strips you set aside for border #1 to that length and sew to the top and bottom of your quilt top.

Measure through the vertical center of your quilt top. From the remaining black fabric cut (2) 5" strips from the length of the fabric, not selvage to selvage. Remove the selvage edges and cut the two strips as long as your quilt top measures vertically. Sew the strips to the side of your quilt top.

Measure through the horizontal center of your quilt top. Cut (2) 5" strips from the length of the black fabric as long as your quilt top measures horizontally. Sew the strips to the side of your quilt top.

Quilting

The areas of black offer an opportunity for fancy quilting, as does the border.

Linda chose to use Perle Cotton to quilt with longer stitches. She matched the colors of the fabrics she used in the blocks and quilted a series of flowers and fluttering butterflies. (This is the Flight in the title in case you thought there was a mistake in spelling!) Linda clearly had fun with her quilting designs and I hope you do, too.

Binding

From the remaining black fabric, cut enough 2" to 2 1/2" strips (depending on the batting you use and how wide you like your bindings) that, when sewn together end to end (following the instructions beginning on page 10), will equal the outside measurement of your quilt top, about 190 inches. Depending on the length of your black fabric piece, you may need (4) strips.

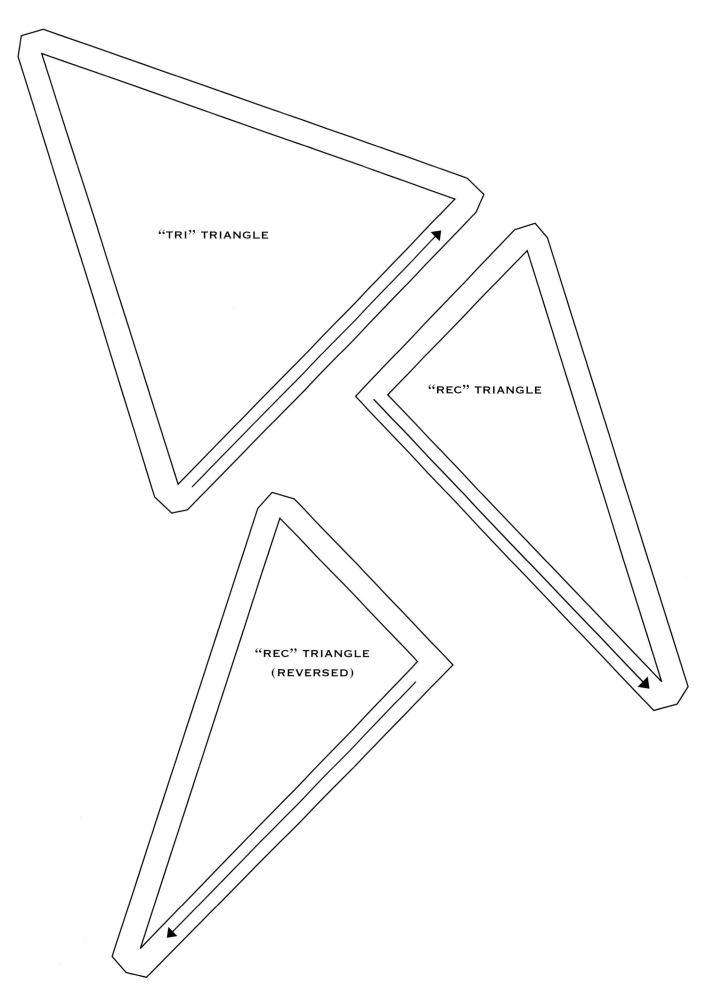

"TRI" TRIANGLE

"REC" TRIANGLE

"REC" TRIANGLE
(REVERSED)

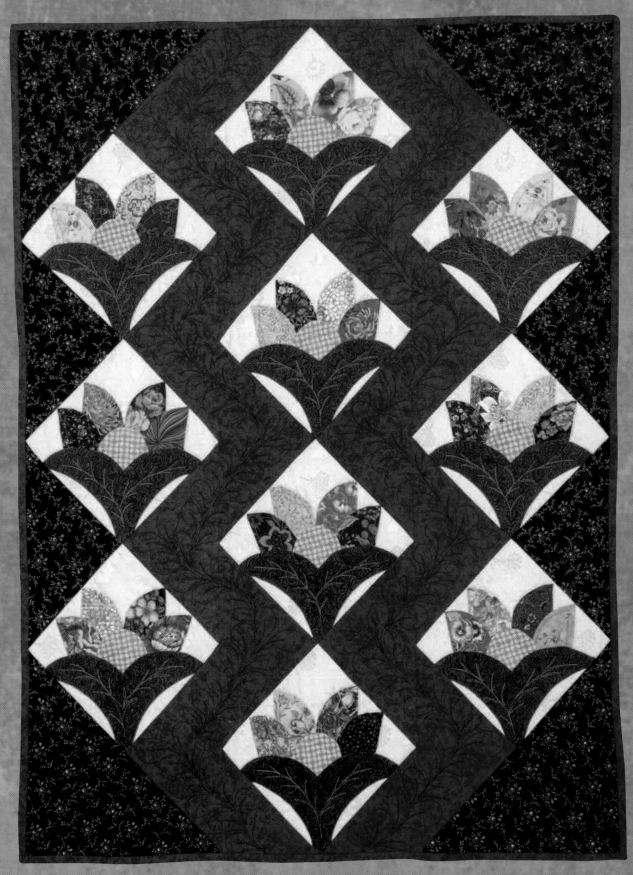

FIELD OF PAINTED DAISIES • 30" x 35"
Made by Cindy Miller, Olathe, Ks. and quilted by Lynne Zeh, Lenexa, Ks.

Fabric

3/4 yard for block background
3/8 yard green for leaves
1/8 yard textured gold for flower centers
1/8 yard each of 8-10 multi-colored floral print
    fabrics for flowers (the more the merrier)
3/4 yard red print for setting triangles
3/8 yard black print for setting triangles
1 1/3 yards for backing
1/3 yard red print for binding

Cutting Instructions

There are a variety of ways to make this block; pieced by hand or machine, fusible appliqué and machine stitched, invisible machine appliqué and hand appliqué. Choose the method you like the best and cut your fabrics accordingly. Following are the cutting instructions for the hand appliqué methods.

Block background: Cut (3) 8 1/2" strips. Sub-cut (10) 8 1/2" squares. (The background squares are cut oversized. When the appliqué is complete, the blocks will be trimmed down to 7 1/2" square.)

Red setting triangles: Cut (2) 11" strips. Sub-cut (4) 11" squares and cut diagonally in both directions for (16) 1/4-square triangles. Cut (2) 6" squares and cut diagonally once for (4) 1/2-square triangles. (These triangles are purposely cut oversized. When the strips are sewn together, you will have enough to trim away and make your strips uniform in size.)

Black setting triangles: Cut (1) 11" strip. Sub-cut (3) 11" squares. Cut (2) of the squares diagonally for (4) 1/2-square triangles. Cut the remaining square diagonally in both directions for (4) 1/4-square triangles.

Constructing the blocks

Using the same green for the leaves of each flower and the same gold center for each flower will tie the blocks together. Mixing up the fabrics in the petals will create the scrappy look for this quilt.

Years ago, I think one would have pieced this block. I recommend the technique of "piecing the appliqué" for these blocks, described on page 7, however, for easier work. You could easily create one set of freezer paper templates and use them for all ten of the blocks. Once the entire flower is pieced, appliqué the unit to the background and trim the block to 7 1/2" square.

Remember, you are only cutting seam allowance for the edges that will be appliquéd. The edges that act as background will not be trimmed until after the seam is appliquéd. You will need to leave extra seam allowance for the edges that serve as background to an adjacent piece. Appliqué one piece to the next, building the flower unit without benefit of the background block. When the unit is complete, appliqué the unit to the background block. Trim the background out from behind the appliqué to eliminate that extra layer of fabric, making quilting easier.

Putting it All Together

Refer to the photograph of the quilt for block and setting triangle placement. You will be sewing three strips to complete this quilt top. The placement of the red or black triangles will define the overall design. The center strip begins and ends with red half-square triangles. Red quarter-square triangles are sewn to the edges of the on-point blocks so the straight-of-grain sides of the triangles form the outer edge of the strip. The side strips are sewn with red quarter-square triangles on the inner edge of the strip and the black quarter-square triangles on the outer, forming with the large half-square triangles in the outer corners a "border" of sorts.

The red binding will "frame" the design and make quite a difference. (We contemplated a binding from the same fabric as the outside triangles, but the whole thing just fell flat.)

Quilting

There are a multitude of quilting designs that would enhance your quilt and the setting triangles certainly offer plenty of space for these designs.

Cindy's machine quilter, Lynne Zeh, created a feather that meanders over the red streaks of lightning. She quilted veins in the leaves and "outlined" about 3/8" inside each of the petals. The outside triangles have chevron designs, bringing the eye into the center of the quilt, back to the flowers.

Binding

Cut (4) strips between 2 1/8" wide to 2 1/2" wide. The loft of your batting and the seam allowance you sew with will determine the width of the strip. Sew the strips together, end-to-end (following the instructions for binding beginning on page 10), and press the seams open to reduce bulk. Fold the strip lengthwise, wrong side in, and sew to the quilted top, fold the finished edge to the back and stitch to secure.

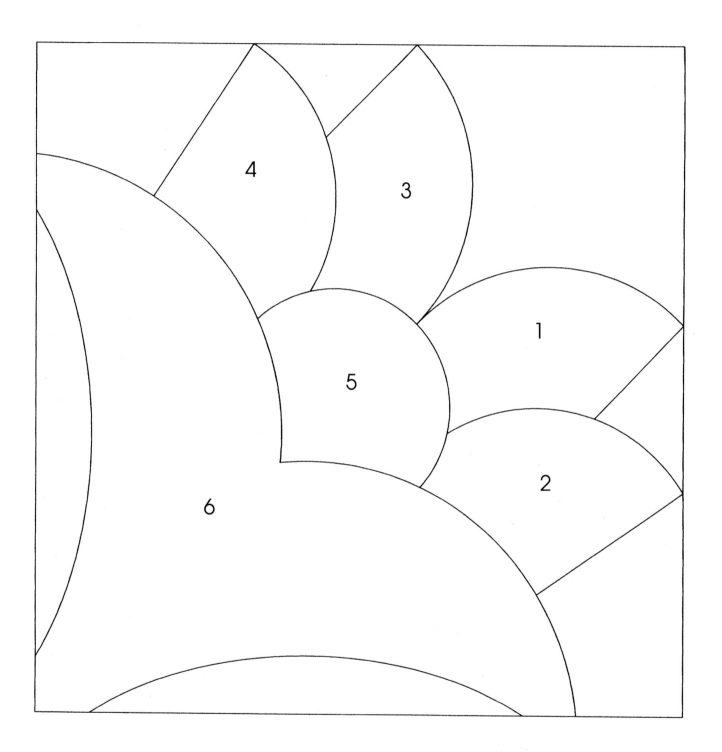

FEATHERED STAR • 55" x 55"
Made by Nancy Khu, Stilwell, Ks. and quilted by Freda Smith, Kansas City, Ks.

Fabric

- 2 1/8 yards red for stars and binding
- 2 1/2 yards white for background, sashing and border
- 1/3 yard medium green for appliqué leaves and stems
- 1/8 yard gold for appliqué flowers
- 1/8 yard deep burgundy red for appliqué flowers
- 3 1/3 yards for backing

2" finished block half-square triangles on a Roll Paper – preprinted foundations for easily making half-square triangle units, available at your local quilt shop

Cutting Instructions for the Star Blocks

All strips are cut selvage to selvage, unless otherwise noted. Cutting instructions are based on 40 usable inches of fabric per strip.

From red fabric

- Cut (1) 10" strip. Sub-cut (4) 10" squares for the appliqué. Once the appliqué is complete, you will trim the blocks to square.
- Cut (2) 2 3/8" strips. Sub-cut (32) 2 3/8" squares.
- Cut (2) 4 3/4" strips. Sub-cut (16) 4 3/4" squares. Cut each square diagonally for (32) 1/2-square triangles to be used in the star points.
- Cut (3) 2 3/8" strips. Sub-cut (32) diamonds. The first cut of the strip at the end of the strip should be at a 45-degree angle. Measuring a parallel 2 3/8" from the first cut, make a second cut for the first diamond. Each cut will be the same until you have cut the complete strip into diamonds. Each strip should yield about (11) diamonds.

From white fabric

- Remove the selvages and from the length of the fabric cut 57 inches. Cut (6) 2 1/2" x 57" strips and set aside. From the remainder, cut (1) 12 3/4" strip. Sub-cut (4) 12 3/4" squares. Cut each of the squares diagonally in both directions for a total of (16) 1/4-square triangles for the sides of the blocks.
- Cut (4) 6 7/8" strips. Sub-cut (16) 6 7/8" squares for the corners of the blocks.
- Cut (3) 2 3/4" strips. Sub-cut (32) 2 3/4" squares.
- Cut the (32) squares diagonally once for (64) 1/2-square triangles for feathers.

Half-square Triangle Units for the Feathers

- Cut (1) 12" strip from the red and (1) 12" strip from the white. Remove the selvages from the strips. Cut (6) 6" x 12" rectangles from each strip. Cut (6) segments of the 1/2-square triangle paper, 2 squares by 4 squares. (This should measure about 6" x 11 1/2".) Following the directions that came with the triangle paper, make a total of (96) red and white 1/2-square triangle units.
- Press the seam allowances toward the red fabric. Each unit should measure 2 1/2" square at this point. Trim each of the units to measure 2 3/8" square.

Appliqué Blocks

Use your favorite method of appliqué or one of the methods described in this book. The template I have provided for the appliqué is drawn for hand appliqué but since it is symmetrical, you will be able to use it "as is" for fusible machine appliqué, too. The numbering on the shapes is your stitching sequence.

Once you have completed the appliqué, place the blocks, right side down, onto a clean fluffy terrycloth towel and press. Set aside until all the Units A and the Units B are constructed. The actual dimension of the units will tell you what size to trim the appliqué blocks.

The picture of the appliqué center is on page 45.

Constructing the blocks

This Feathered Star is a 9-patch block, consisting of 3 units: the (4) corner squares, the (4) side triangles and the appliquéd center square. Breaking the block down and constructing the units makes this block rather easy.

Unit A: *This is actually the easier of the two units to construct, so I recommend you get started here.*
Begin by laying all the elements out on your sewing table to get a sense of triangle direction. Refer to the photograph. The first time I ever made this block I merrily sewed all the pieces into pairs and then sadly had to remove the stitches from half of them because they were oriented wrong. The triangles on the one side of the corner square are opposite the triangles on the adjacent side.

Once you have the unit elements arranged, stack the elements together and chain piece, sewing all sixteen units at the same time. Not only is it a time saver, but it is a great thread saver, too. When sewing the feathers to the background square, press the seam allowance toward the background square.

Unit A

Unit B: *Now that you have all of the Units A completed, these will be a breeze.*
Referring to the diagram, lay out all the elements on your sewing table, making sure the triangles are in the correct direction. Chain piece, sewing all sixteen units at the same time. As you add the background triangle to the feathers, I would recommend you partially sew the seam, leaving the seam to the white triangles open until you sew the rows together. Press the seam allowance toward the background triangle.

With the appliqué centers complete and the A and B units complete, you're ready to construct the four blocks. Lay the sections out on your sewing table as before. Notice, this block is, in essence, a nine-patch. When you sew the A Units to the B Units in row one and row three, sew the seam to complete the feathers. Then go back and finish the seam between the feathers and the background triangle in unit B.

Unit B

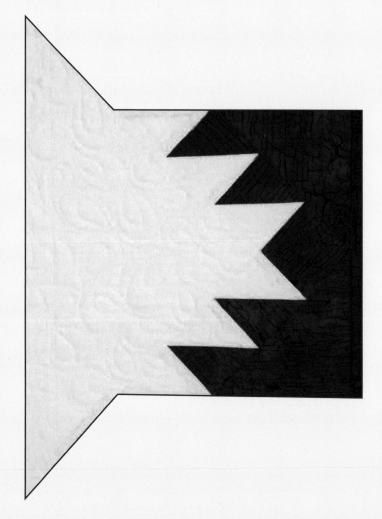

Sew the three rows together, pressing the seam allowances toward the center row.

Putting it All Together

Measure your blocks. In a perfect world, they will measure 25 1/4" square. From the (6) 2 1/2" x 57" reserved white fabric strips, cut (1) 2 1/2" strip. Sub-cut (2) 2 1/2" x 25 1/4" strips (or 2 1/2" x your block's measurement). Sew a block to either side of the strips. Measure the length of these new units and cut another 2 1/2" strip, trimming it to this new measurement. Sew the two rows together to complete the center of your quilt top.
Measure through the vertical center of the quilt top and cut (2) 2 1/2" strips from the length of the white fabric. Trim the strips to the vertical measurement and sew to the sides of the quilt top.

Measure through the horizontal center of the quilt top and cut (2) 2 1/2" strips from the length of the white fabric. Trim the strips to this measurement and sew to the top and bottom of the quilt top.

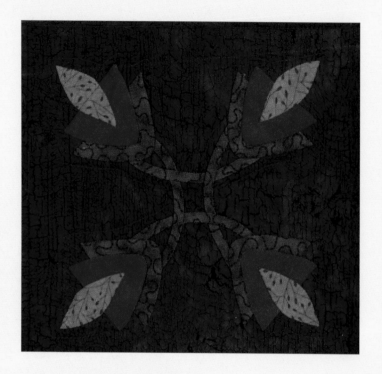

Quilting

Freda kept the feather theme in mind while she quilted an all-over feathery design in the background. She outlined the appliqué and quilted "in the ditch" to highlight the star. Matching the thread to the fabric let the stars shine while enhancing the piecing with quilting.

Binding

Cut (6) 2 1/4" – 2 1/2" strips from the red fabric. Sew the strips together, end-to-end (following the instructions beginning on page 11), with a diagonal seam and press the seam allowances open to eliminate bulk. Fold the strip in half lengthwise, wrong side in and apply to the edge of the quilt top, raw edges aligned and mitering the corners. Turn the finished edge to the back and stitch by hand to the back of the quilt.

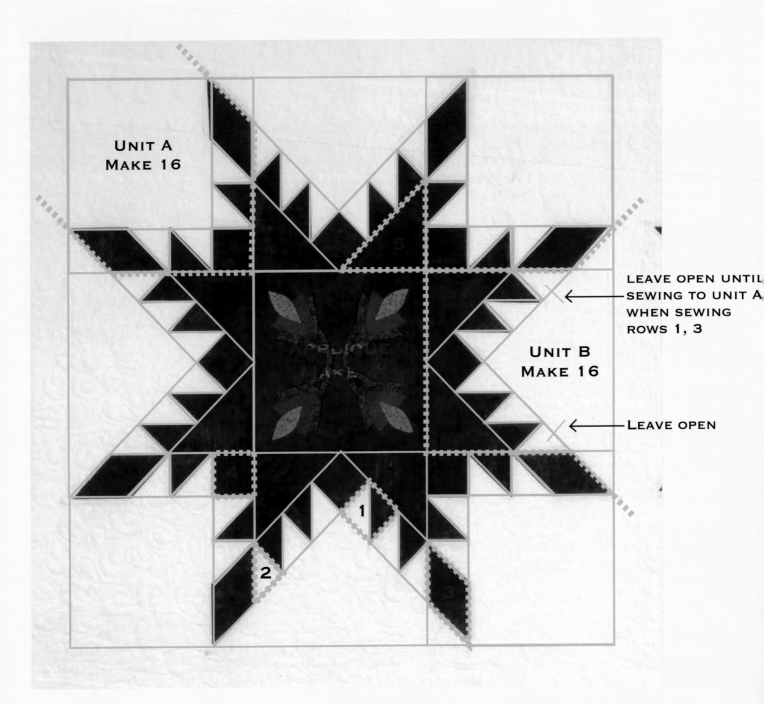

UNIT A
MAKE 16

LEAVE OPEN UNTIL SEWING TO UNIT A WHEN SEWING ROWS 1, 3

UNIT B
MAKE 16

LEAVE OPEN

1. Make 96
2. Cut 64
3. Cut 32
4. Cut 32
5. Cut 32

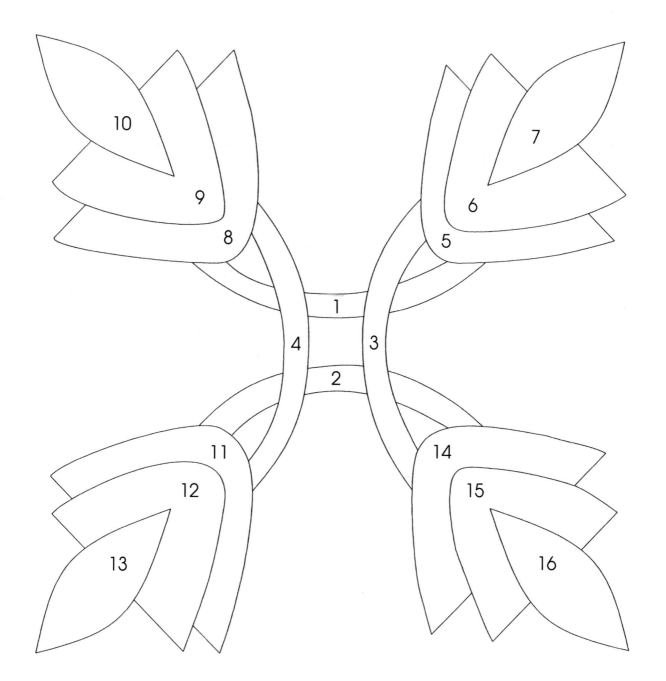

PRAIRIE STAR • 95" X 95"
Made by Kathy Delaney and machine quilted by Kelly Ashton, Overland Park, Ks.

If you are the sort of quilter who routinely just looks at the pictures and does not read the pattern, I suggest that, with this project, you change your routine. I suggest that you refer to the written words of this pattern regularly. While the Lone Star can be accomplished with success, there really are specific steps that must be taken to ensure that success.

When I created my first Lone Star quilt, I did not have a pattern but I did have a little constant "buzz" in my ear guiding me, in the person of Liz Porter at a weekend retreat. I am very grateful to Liz for her help. While I may very well have arrived at the same success, I know that Liz helped me get there without pain. For this I am very grateful! Let the words I write on these pages be your "buzz," guiding you to success.

Fabric Requirements
Star Points – 9 fabrics
The fabrics needed for the star points are listed below, beginning with the diamond at the outside point. When purchasing, you might consider making a list to include a descriptive phrase of the fabric for each position in the star point. When referring to each fabric in the pattern instructions, I will only use the letter.

A – 1/3 yard
B – 1/3 yard
C – 1/3 yard
D – 1/2 yard
E – 1/2 yard
F – 5/8 yard
G – 1/2 yard
H – 1/2 yard
J – 1/3 yard

Background – 2 1/2 yards
Appliqué
  Flower petals – 1/2 yard
  Stems and leaves – 1/2 yard
  Flower center – 1/3 yard
Border – 3 yards (this gives you some flexibility in width)
Binding – 3/4 yard
Backing – 5 1/2 yards

1 1/2 yards light paper-backed fusible web for machine appliqué

Preparing Your Fabric
You may wish to pre-wash your fabrics. I did not. I wanted the sizing in the fabric to help me. I suggest that you test your fabrics for crocking – dye color rubbing off the surface of the fabric – and bleeding – color running onto adjacent fabrics – before you begin, to save yourself some heartache later.

Cutting Instructions
From each of the fabrics listed below, using your rotary cutting tools, cut 3-inch strips. All cuts should be made across the grain of the fabric, from selvage to selvage, unless otherwise noted. It is very important to be as accurate as possible in every step of this quilt top, so plan to take plenty of time to make these cuts. (The yardage has been figured so that you should be able to get one extra strip out of each of the fabrics if you make a mistake.)

A – cut (3) 3" strips
B – cut (3) 3" strips
C – cut (3) 3" strips
D – cut (4) 3" strips
E – cut (5) 3" strips
F – cut (6) 3" strips
G – cut (5) 3" strips
H – cut (4) 3" strips
I – cut (3) 3" strips

From the background fabric, cut (4) 22" squares. Cut (1) 33" square; cut the square diagonally in both directions for (4) 1/4-square triangles.

Preparing Your Strip Sets
Below you will find a grid that represents one of your star points. Each segment of the grid has a letter. The letters, remember, represent your fabrics. The numbers across the top of the grid represent a strip set. For each row, you will make a strip set that will include six of your fabrics in the order listed. For instance, Strip Set #1 includes fabrics **f**, **g**, **h**, **i**, **a** and **b**. You will make a total of 6 strip sets.

If you are very accurate in your stitching, you will get all the strips you will need from each strip set.

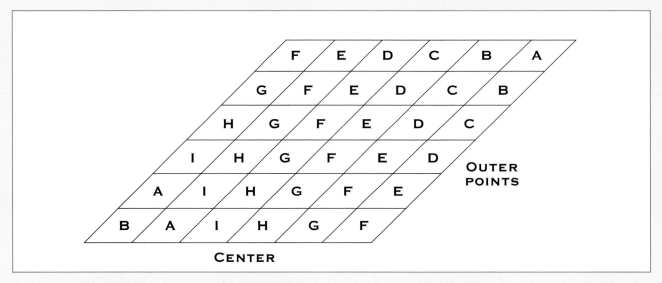

Begin by arranging each of your 3" strips into sets in the order listed on the grid. For instance, Strip Set #1 will have fabric "f" on top and fabric "b" will be on the bottom of the pile. Pin the set together with a pin so you won't lose anything and write #1 on a small piece of paper and pin it to the set. Arrange each set, from top to bottom, and label each set with its corresponding number. (Organization and accuracy are everything in this project!)

Once you have organized your strip sets, you are ready to sew them together. You are probably familiar with the process of sewing strips together to make a strip set, beginning your ends evenly. If you sew this way for the Lone Star you will not have enough fabric to cut all your strips and you will end up wasting a lot of fabric. Instead, you will be staggering the ends to form a "step" so that when you sub-cut the strip sets into new strips you'll have enough fabric with no waste.

The top strip from your pile is placed on the table in front of you horizontally. Fold the upper left corner down, forming a triangle, and note where that fold begins. It should be right at 3 inches. At this point, place the left edge (right sides together) of the second strip on your pile, aligning it with the right edge of the first strip. Sew a very accurate 1/4" seam the length of the strip. (If you are in doubt regarding the accuracy of your 1/4" seam, cut 2

rectangles of fabric 2 1/2" x 4 1/2". Sew the two rectangles together along the 2 1/2" side with your best 1/4" seam. Press your seam to one side and measure the unit. It should measure 4 1/2" x 4 1/2".) Add strip #3 in the same manner to the right of strip #2 and so on. The diagram below will help you. Hold off pressing your seams until all of the strips are added and then press all the seams open. This is different from your normal patchwork but believe me, it will make a better star point, eliminating bulk at the intersections.

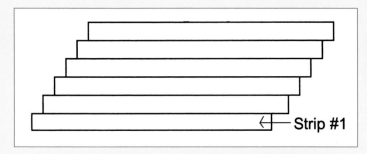

While the left "step" should be kept as even as possible, (by folding down the corner to find the spot to line up the next piece), the right inverted step may be uneven. The length of your strips will determine this. Not all fabrics are the same width. It is important that you try to begin sewing your 3" strip 3 inches from the end each time.

Press the seams open, taking care not to distort your strip sets. "Pressing" is the operative word here. **It is very important that you do not iron, but press! (I cannot stress this too much! Take your time!)** I found that if I lay my strip set vertically over my ironing board instead of horizontally, I did not get the "smile" or "rainbow effect" so very common after pressing strip sets. (There are differing opinions regarding the use of steam. I use steam. But you must remember to press and not iron! Steam will help you **iron** in a distortion – the "smile" – while steam will help you **press** a crisp seam. I cannot stress enough the importance of pressing and not ironing!) Once I had all my seam allowances pressed open, I went back over the strip set (again, pressing, not ironing) a few times with spray starch, starching both sides. You cannot make your strip sets too stiff, so feel free to be generous with the spray starch. Just remember – **PRESS, DON'T IRON!** Be sure to pin the strip set's number back onto your strip set as you finish pressing. I found that if I pinned the number to the far left upper corner of the first (bottom) "step," I was able to keep track of the number and didn't have to remove it while I was sub-cutting my strips.

When you have made all 6 of your strip sets and pressed the seams, you are ready to sub-cut into cross strips. Place your 24" rotary cutting ruler on the left side of your strip set so that the 45 degree line is perfectly lined up with one of seams and the left edge of the ruler is as far left as necessary so that you can cut off the steps without cutting into your strip set any farther than necessary. Cut off the steps and discard, keeping the number to place on the pile when you've completed cutting. If you can cut with both your left hand as well as right, you're lucky. You won't have to move your mat. However, if you can only cut with your right hand, walk around to the other side of the table to make this first cut or turn your mat. The idea is to disturb your strip set as little as possible. Lifting the strip set to turn it will stretch the bias edge.

Very carefully line up the 3-inch mark on your ruler along the edge you just cut. Again, the 45-degree line is perfectly parallel to one of the seams. Cut the strip. **WITH AS LITTLE HANDLING AS POSSIBLE, SET THIS NEW STRIP ASIDE.** Your strip is now considered "on the bias" and could very easily get stretched out of shape. If you pressed with enough spray starch, you will have gone a long way toward eliminating the possibility of stretching the strip. Handling as little as possible will also help! Continue cutting 3" strips until you have 8 strips. Be very careful lining up your ruler or you may find that you can only get 7 strips. You will have to use some of your excess to create another strip if this happens. You may find that you have to re-cut that left edge after cutting every other strip or so that your angle stays a true 45 degrees. The straighter the set stays in pressing, the less truing the edge you'll have to do.

Remember that accuracy is what makes this project a success! When you have cut all 8 strips, carefully pin the number to the pile and set aside. Repeat with the other 5 strip sets until you have all of your strips sub-cut.

Sewing Your Star Points

Starting with a bias strip from strip set #1 and then #2 and so forth, stacking one of each of the 6 strips into a pile. #1 will be on top and #6 will be on the bottom. You should have 8 complete sets of these strips. Each set represents one of the star points.

Again, starting with the top-most strip, right side up on the table, lay the second strip, right sides

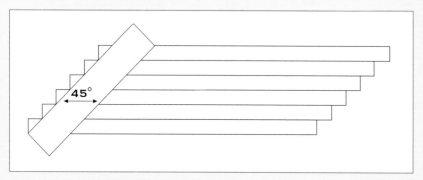

together, on top. Until you get a rhythm and can really gauge 3/8 of an inch by eye, you will need to pin each and every seam intersection. Remember, too, that you need to treat each of these pieced strips very gingerly so as not to stretch any part. This is very important to the success of this project. Any stretching must be handled by easing the edge.

To pin an intersection, stick a pin straight down through the fabric at the first seam, 1/4" from the raw edge. Continue sticking the pin straight down through the fabric of the strip underneath at the seam, 1/4" from the raw edge. With the pin just poking straight down through both seams, use another pin to carefully connect the two strips together, just to the left of the vertical pin. By pinning to the left of the intersection, you will be less likely to shift the position while sewing. Remove the vertical pin and go on to the next intersection. Repeat for each of the intersections. Eventually, I think you'll get the hang of the fact that when the angled seams cross just at the right spot there is a 1/8" gap between the ends of the two seams. (1) If you sew from seam intersection to seam intersection, aligning the edges as you go, you will probably give up pinning and discover you're just as accurate. (2)

Sew the seam carefully with a very accurate 1/4" seam allowance. Sew all the strips to make the star point unit before pressing. Pressing will be done by blocking the star points.

On a large piece of muslin or freezer paper, draw a line 21" long along one edge with a permanent marker. Draw a line parallel to the first, 2 1/2" from the first. Repeat these lines until you have six rows. Draw a line from one end at a 45-degree angle. 21" long. Draw a line parallel to this line, 2 1/2" from the first. Repeat these lines until you have six rows. You might have to lengthen some of the lines so your grid forms a diamond, replicating your star points. Finally, draw a line around the whole shape 1/4" from the original lines. Extend all the grid lines so they cross this outer edge. You want to be able to see where those grid lines intersect the outer edge.

Place the grid on your ironing board and secure. If you used freezer paper, iron it right to the ironing board surface. Starting with the top edge, pin one of your star points so the outer edge of the fabric matches the line on the ironing board. Use a glass-head quilting pin at every seam and match the seam to the lines that intersect the outer line of the grid. (Place the pins so they are almost flat to the ironing board surface and the glass head is outside the circumference of the diamond. Be sure you are using glass-head pins and not plastic.) Continue pinning all the way around the star point, matching the seams with the grid lines, pinning the seam allowance open, and the outer raw edge of the star point with the outside edge of the drawing. You may have to stretch in some places and ease in others. Just be sure to match the lines in the grid with the seams.

With a steam iron, press the seam allowances open, being careful to press with an up and down motion. This will ease the fabric where you eased it and set it where you stretched while opening the seam allowances. The steam will reactivate the starch and set the star point, making sewing the star together much easier.

When you have successfully completed the 8 star point units, you are ready to put your star together! Determine which end of the star point unit is the outer point and which becomes the center of the star by pinning them up on your design wall or laying them all out on the floor to study. Flip the points and see what happens. You will sew the star together in segments with the background setting squares and triangles.

Preparing Your Background

Once you have sewn all of your star points, you are ready to cut your background squares and quarter-square triangles. Notice that each star point has a straight edge and a bias edge. I suggest that you handle those bias edges very gingerly to avoid stretching.

I like to cut my setting squares and triangles over-sized. This allows me to choose between squaring up the center of the quilt by trimming a 1/4" seam allowance all the way around or floating the star a bit. It is your choice. Floating the star, that is creating a space with background fabric between the star points and the frame, whether it is a border or just the binding, tends to let the star stand out just a bit more. In Prairie Star, however, I did not float the star.

Sew the seams that connect to the triangle first. The seam that joins the two star points together in the star center should be sewn last. Always begin

at the narrow point of the star and sew toward the inside corner, stopping and back stitching 1/4" from the end of the seam. Feel free to use lots of pins to inset the background, taking great care that you don't stretch any of the bias edges (star points as well as side triangles). Plan on sewing just one side seam of the star points and 1/4-square triangles at a time – no pivoting at the inside corner. Begin stitching from the outside points and work into the inside corner. Do not try to pivot at the inside corner to sew both seams. If your 1/4" seams have been accurate, you will have room to trim excess. Press the seam allowances away from the star points.

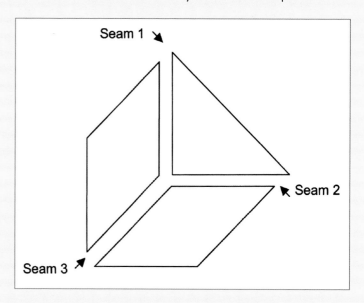

Sew two of the star point units to a corner square in the same way you did the 1/4-square triangle and press the seam allowance away from the star point. Again, begin stitching at the outside point and sew toward the inside corner. Repeat with the second two units for the two halves of the star. Sew the remaining two squares to the right hand star point of each of the star halves (opposite corners of the quilt center).

To sew the two halves together, sew the background square to the corresponding star point, working from the outside point toward the inside corner. Sew the other background corner square to the remaining star point, again sewing from the outside point toward the inside corner. Press the seam allowances away from the star points.

Sew the center by pinning the seam intersections as you did when you sewed the rows of the star points. Begin in the center and sew toward the corner squares. By sewing from the center out you are more likely to match the center where all the seams come together. Press the seam open, taking great care not to stretch. After all this work, you do not want to create a volcano in the center!

At this point, trim the excess to square up your center, either leaving just 1/4" seam allowance, or floating your star.

Preparing Your Appliqué

The flowers, stems and leaves of the appliqué were all machine stitched on my quilt. However, if you prefer to do hand appliqué it would look just as wonderful! Hand appliqué artists may be tempted to stitch the appliqué onto the corner squares and side triangles before they inset them into the Lone Star. I would advise that you don't do that. Go ahead and inset the background into the Lone Star and then do your appliqué. It will be a little more awkward, I know, but you run the risk of stretching those bias edges. If you choose to appliqué before you cut the triangles apart, you run the risk of distorting the size of that square due to your stitch tension. Since accuracy is so very important to the success of this project, I strongly recommend that you do the appliqué after the Lone Star is all put together.

The patterns have already been reversed for fusible appliqué. Trace each element of the appliqué separately onto the paper side of your fusible web product, leaving about 1/2" between patterns. Follow the directions that came with your fusible product for applying it to the wrong side of your fabric. Cut each piece out along the traced line. Peel the paper backing off the piece and arrange the pieces on your quilt top and fuse, again following the directions with the fusible material. The dotted lines on the pattern indicate the place-ment of the pieces to create the flowers. There are two sizes of the flowers. The larger flower is meant

to go on the corner squares. The smaller flower is designed for the side triangles.

If you are going to hand quilt your *Prairie Star*, you may consider "windowing" your fusible material. By that I mean, trace the pattern onto the paper side of the fusible, leaving the 1/2" between patterns. Before fusing the material to the wrong side of your fabric, cut out the center of the fusible, leaving only about 1/4" all the way around the edge, creating a window. (This lets the appliqué be adhered to the top while you are stitching but there is no stiff glue to try to hand quilt through.) After you fuse the back of your fabric, cut the shape out following the line that you traced. Remove the paper backing only when you are ready to fuse the piece to the quilt top, following the directions that came with your fusible material.

I used a small "blanket" stitch built into my sewing machine. I used the open toed embroidery foot so that I could see where I was going. I used a cotton 50 weight 2-ply thread, matching the color to my appliqué fabrics. If your machine does not have the blanket stitch, you may use a short, narrow zigzag stitch. By using thread to match, your stitches will not show.

Preparing Your Border

When you have completed your Prairie Star and appliqué you will be ready to add the final border. The fabric requirement for the border lets you decide now if you want a 9-inch border for a 91" x 91" quilt top or if you want to make it wider, thus making the quilt top bigger. Either way, the corners are mitered.

Begin by measuring through the vertical center of your Lone Star quilt top. (I know, there is no clear top, just pick a direction and you're set.) To that measurement, add 2 times the width of your border plus 1 inch or more. (You will want to have too much rather than too little and you will be trimming the excess.) Cut four strips, lengthwise along your fabric, this length and as wide as you've decided your border will be. (I used a full 1/4 the width of the fabric for my borders.) Mark the exact center of each strip and mark on the border where the edge of the Lone Star comes (the distance from the center of the Lone Star out to the edge in both directions) on two of them. Pin a border on, using these markings and then ease in the rest. Begin stitching 1/4" from the end and stop stitching 1/4" from the other end, backstitching to secure. Repeat with the border strip and the opposite side of the quilt top.

Measure through the center of your Lone Star horizontally through the quilt. This time you are measuring from the outside edge of one of the applied borders to the outside edge of the other applied border. Mark the exact center of the strips and where the edge of the top comes as you did before. Pin the borders on and begin stitching from the seam that you have just sewn and stop at the other end in the same place, backstitching to secure. You should have the four sides applied but corners that have not yet been sewn.

There are several ways to achieve the mitered corner. Any one of them will give you successful results. Choose your favorite method or you might try the one I use. With right sides together, I make a diagonal fold through one corner of the top. I line up the border strips very evenly along their seams and I pin to secure. Using a ruler, I extend the "line" created by the diagonal fold and mark the diagonal line on the wrong side of the border strip. (1) Beginning at the outside corner and stitching toward the inside of the miter, I stitch along my drawn line. (2) When I open this up I have a perfectly mitered corner. I press the seams open (notice that I "press," I do not "iron") and cut away the excess, leaving a 1/4" seam allowance. (3) I repeat this on the remaining 3 corners.

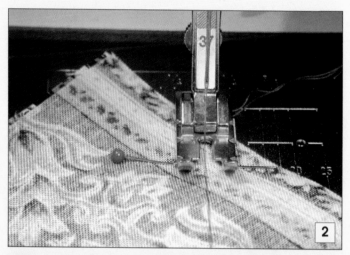

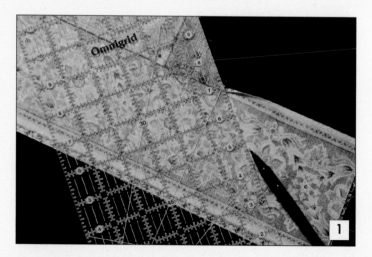

Quilting

There is no single way to design the quilting on any quilt. My quilt, quilted on a long-arm machine, has a terrific feathered wreath in the center of the Lone Star. You may wish to quilt in cross-hatching. Whether by machine or by hand I suggest you avoid stitching through the center of the quilt with 8 crossing lines of quilting. You will very likely end up with a bowl.

Binding

Refer to instructions for binding beginning on page 10.

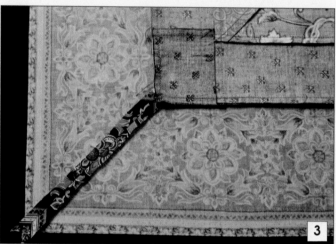

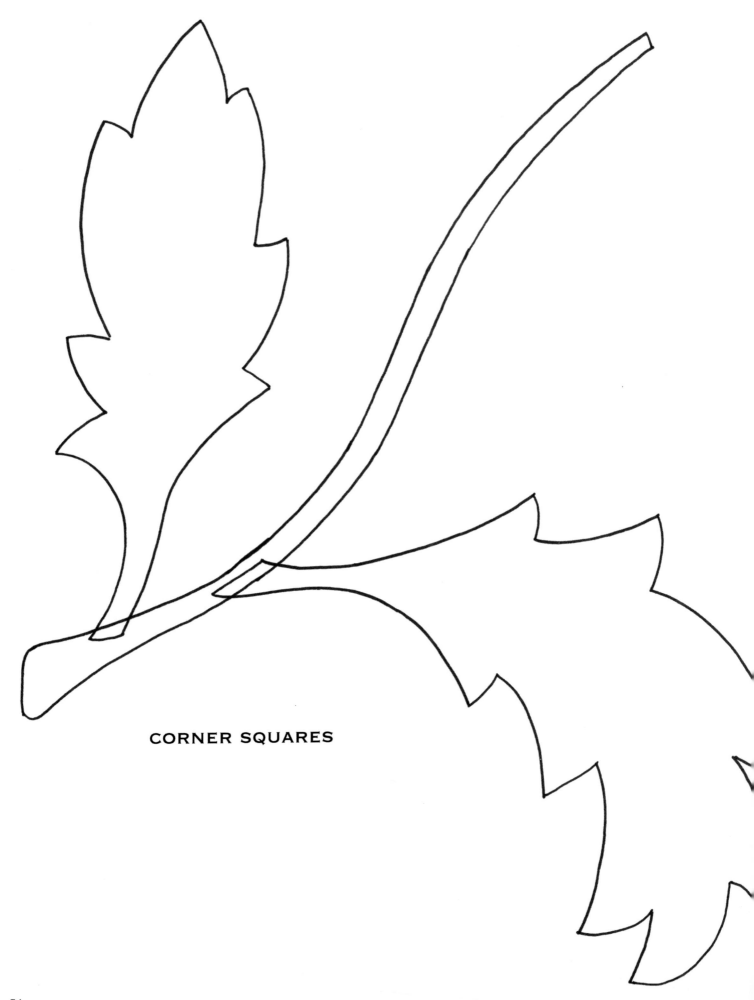

CORNER SQUARES

56

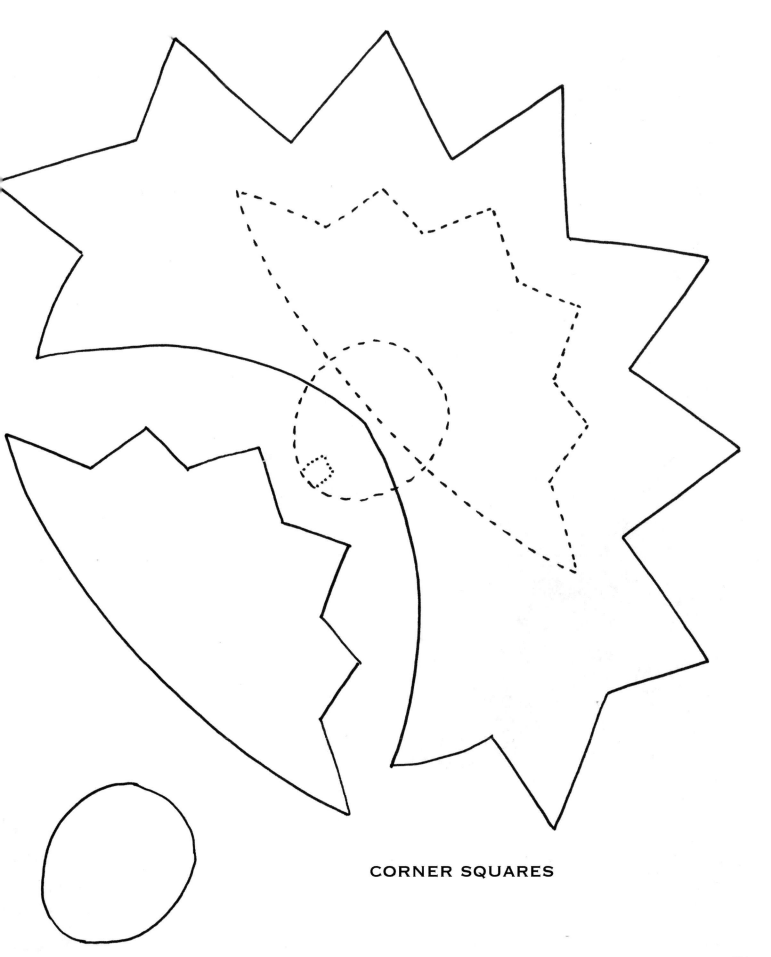

CORNER SQUARES

SIDE TRIANGLE

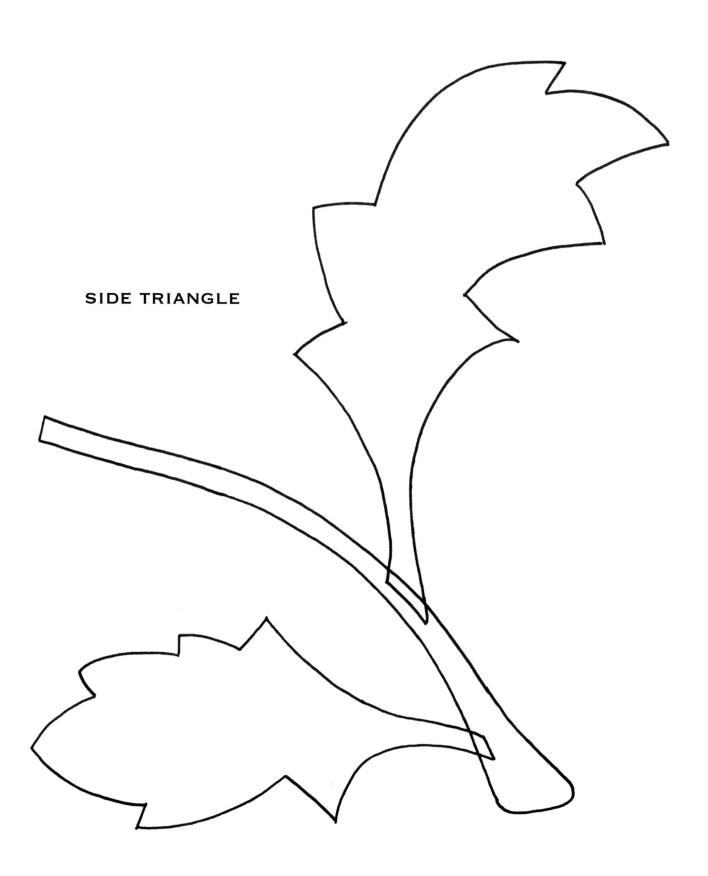

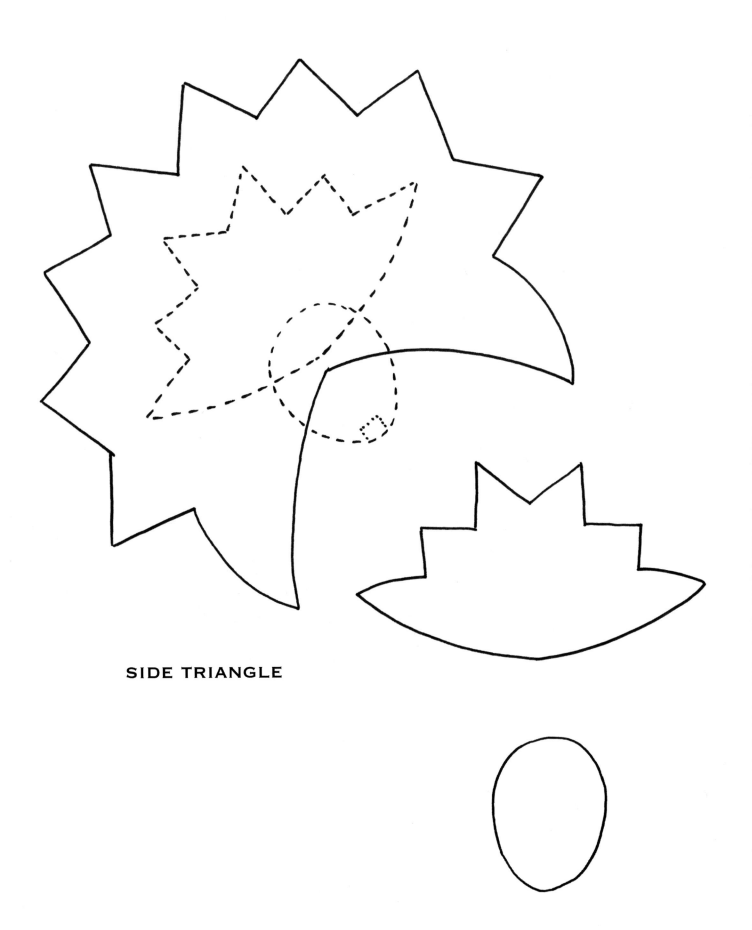

SIDE TRIANGLE

LOVE STAR WALL QUILT • 52" X 52"
Made by Tresa Jones, Seneca, Ks.

Fabric

- 1 1/4 yards red for large diamonds and appliqué
- 1 3/4 yards gold for side triangles, corner squares and appliqué
- 1 7/8 yards green for 4-patch diamonds, appliqué and 1" binding
- 1 3/8 yards cream for 4-patch diamonds, appliquéd diamonds and appliqué
- 3 yards for backing

Appliqué Diamonds

I recommend you cut the diamonds after you complete the appliqué. Because appliqué techniques can distort the block, cut your background pieces larger than the size you need for the quilt. Cut (2) 15" strips. Sub-cut (8) 5" x 7" rectangles. Centering them on the rectangles, appliqué the Love Apples. I recommend you make a template of the diamond for placement purposes. Lightly mark the diamond because once the appliqué is complete the markings may no longer be in the right place.

I also recommend spraying the rectangles with starch with your final pressing. Place the rectangles, right side down, on a clean, fluffy terrycloth towel. Lightly spray the wrong side of the block with a starch or sizing product. Press and repeat. I like to add enough starch that the block is pretty stiff. The starch will help the bias edges stay true as you are handling them in the quilt top construction. Cut the diamonds from the rectangles and set aside.

4-Patch Diamonds

Cut (1) 7" strip from the green fabric and (1) 7" strip from the cream fabric. Lightly spray the strips with a starch or sizing product and press. Repeat a couple of times in order to make the strips fairly stiff. Cut each strip into (2) 3 1/8" strips. Pair a green and cream strip and sew into a set, repeat with the second pair. Press the seam allowance toward the green strip. As you press, take great care that you don't distort the strips and cause a "frown." That is, you want the strip to stay straight, not form a curve.

Align the 45-degree line marked on your rotary cutting ruler with the seam of the strip set and cut the end to form an angle. Continue cutting segments at a 45-degree angle. Each cut will be 3 1/8" from the preceding cut. Periodically you may have to realign the angled edge, depending on how well you pressed the set, to make sure each diamond is a 45-degree diamond. Cut (16) 3 1/8" segments.

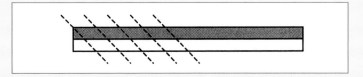

To make the 4-Patch diamonds you will pair two segments as you would for any 4-Patch square. To make sure the intersections are well done, you must remember the angle cut of a 1/4" seam allowance is 3/8". Instead of the raw edges exactly matching as with straight patchwork, there will be a 1/8" difference between the raw edged corner of one seam allowance and the raw edged corner of the matching seam allowance.

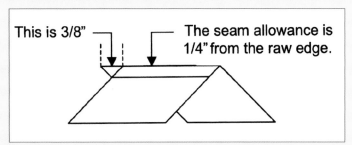

This is 3/8"

The seam allowance is 1/4" from the raw edge.

When you remember the 3/8" your seams will always meet 1/4" from the edge as they are supposed to.

On a piece of freezer paper, draw the diamond shape with a permanent marker and press it to your ironing board. The parallel lines measure 5 3/4" apart. When you have completed the 4-Patch diamonds, pin them to the diamond shape to press. Be sure to use glass head quilting pins and place the pins at an angle from the diamonds, keeping the pin heads to the outside of the diamond. Press with a steam iron to reactivate the starch and set your diamond. In essence you will be "blocking" your 4-Patches to eliminate any distortion that may have occurred while constructing the diamonds.

Red Diamonds
Spray the red fabric with starch and press several times in order make the fabric fairly stiff. Again, this helps maintain the integrity of your bias edges. Cut (6) 5 3/4" strips from the red fabric. Sub-cut (16) 5 3/4" diamonds.

Corner block appliqué
From the gold background fabric, cut (2) 16 1/2" strips. Sub-cut (4) 16 1/2" squares. Refer to the photograph of the quilt and appliqué the Love Apples to the center of the squares. When the appliqué is complete, set the squares aside. Once the star points are made you'll be able to determine what size to trim the squares.

Putting it All Together
Refer to the photograph of the quilt and sew the star points. Each point is made from (2) red diamonds, (1) 4-Patch diamond and (1) appliqué diamond. Press the seam allowances open to eliminate bulk.

On another piece of freezer paper, draw another diamond. This time the parallel lines should be 11" apart. Pin the star points to the diamond shape and press to block just as you did for the 4-Patch diamonds.

Measure the side of a diamond from the points 1/4" in from edge. Add 3/4" and that is the size to cut the corner appliquéd squares. Usually I would recommend you set the oversized squares in and then trim, but doing that would take your appliqué out of the center placement. I have already added a 1/4" "fudge factor" so you can still straighten the edges once the top is complete.

Cut a 22" square from the gold background fabric and cut it diagonally twice for (4) 1/4-square triangles.

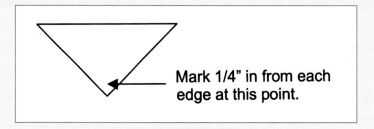

Mark 1/4" in from each edge at this point.

Sew a star point to a triangle as the diagram shows below, sewing from the outside point toward the center, stopping and backstitching at the 1/4" mark. The second seam will be sewing the second diamond to the triangle, stopping and backstitching at the 1/4" mark. The third seam will be the two diamonds together, always sewing from the outside point toward the center. Press the seam allowances away from the star points.

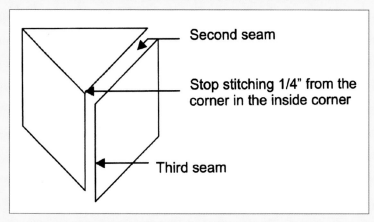

Second seam

Stop stitching 1/4" from the corner in the inside corner

Third seam

Mark the inside corner of the corner appliquéd blocks. Refer to the quilt picture for placement and orientation of the appliqué. Set the corner blocks just as you did the triangles, sewing from the star point toward the center. At this point you will have two halves of the star and two corner blocks. Sew a corner block to the far right star point of each of the segments.

Now sew the two halves together. Sew the corner squares to the remaining star points, completing the star. Always sew from the outside point toward the center and press the seam allowance away from the star point.

To stitch the center seam, begin stitching from the center of the seam out to the edge, sewing one half of the center seam. Begin again in the center and stitch out to the edge, sewing the second half of the center seam. By stitching from the center out, you are more likely to make that center point where all eight seams meet come together accurately. Press the center seam allowance open to eliminate bulk.

Once all the background pieces are set into the star, you may trim the outside edges of the quilt top to even them, leaving a 1/4" seam allowance all the way around.

Quilting
Tresa hand quilted her quilt with a cream thread. She quilted around each of the appliqué shapes and an echoing straight line in the background every inch, radiating out from the star points. In the star points she quilted in the ditch and echoed every inch from the inside corner of the red diamonds and a secondary grid within the 4-patch diamonds.

Binding
Tresa bound her quilt with a traditional 1/4" binding. However, if you want to make a more definite frame, try a 1" finished binding which will frame this quilt taking the place of an added border. To make the 1" binding cut (6) 6 1/4" strips and sew end to end for a continuous strip. I recommend a bias seam, pressing the seam allowances open to eliminate bulk.

Square the quilt and the corners and trim the excess batting and backing from the quilt, leaving 3/4" excess of batting and backing. Either use a rotary cutting ruler and a marker to establish the edge and cut with scissors or cut the excess with a rotary cutter. When you sew the binding, you will sew 1" from this edge, but you will be sewing 1/4" into the quilt top.

Fold the strip in half, the length of the strip, with wrong side in, and press. Attach the binding as you usually do, mitering the corners, sewing with a 1" seam allowance. Turn the right side to the back and hand stitch the finished edge to the back of the quilt, covering the machine stitching.

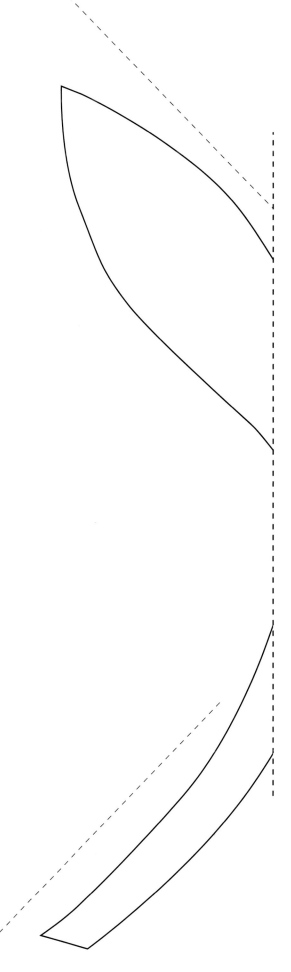

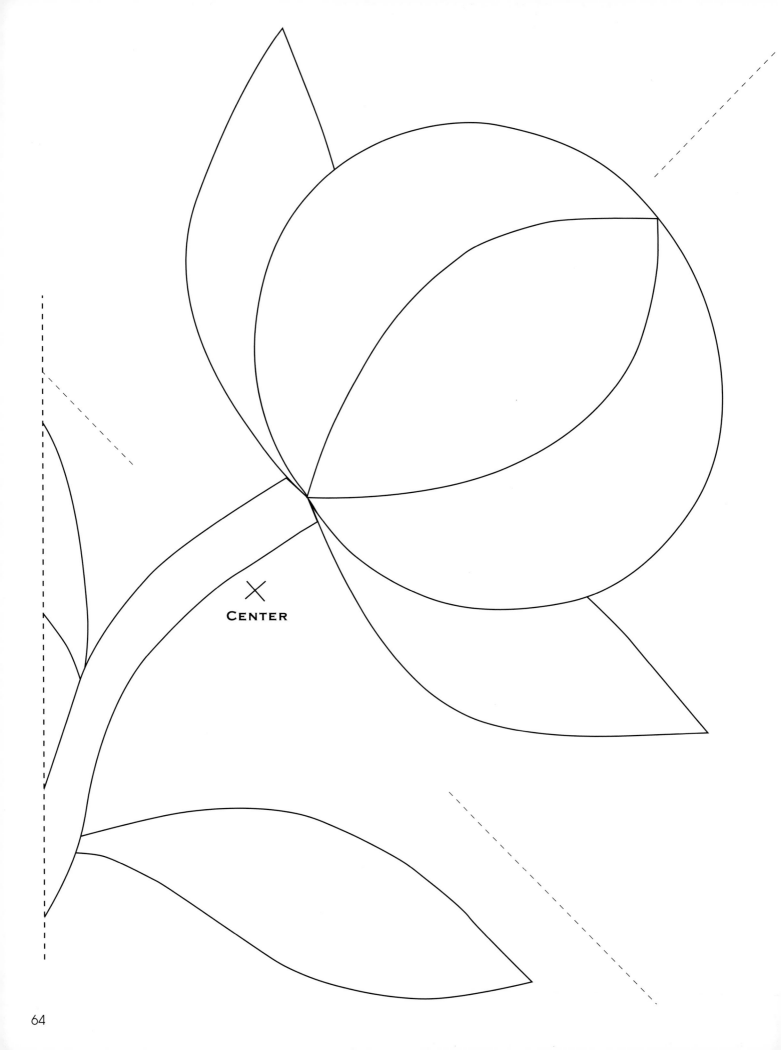

CENTER

SUNFLOWER FIELDS • 75" x 75"
Made by Barb Fife, Overland Park, Ks. and quilted by Alice Scott, Lenexa, Ks.

This pattern is designed in two sizes, 75" square and 50" square. The larger quilt has 18-inch blocks and the smaller has 12-inch blocks. The fabric requirements and the cutting instructions for the smaller quilt are listed in brackets. The directions for constructing the quilt are the same for both sizes. You might go through the pattern and highlight the measurements that pertain to the size of quilt you're planning to make.

Fabric

    3 7/8 (2 1/4) yards red background
    1 3/4 (3/4) yards gold #1 for flowers
    1 3/4 (3/4) yards gold #2 for flowers
    3 1/8 (1 3/8) yards dark green for stems
       and 1 1/2" (1") binding
    5/8 (1/3) yard brown texture for flower centers
    3/4 (1/4) yard medium green for leaves
    4 1/2 (3 1/2) yards for backing

Cutting Instructions

Before cutting the golds or cutting the background, I recommend you spray starch and iron. Turn it over and repeat. The more starch you put into the fabric, the more stable the fabric will remain when you cut the bias edges of the diamonds and the 1/4-square triangles. This will make sewing the bias edges together easier.

From red background cut (16) 3 1/8" ((12) 2 1/4") strips, sub-cut (192) 3 1/8" ((192) 2 1/4") squares.
Cut (4) 9 1/2" ((3) 6 1/2") strips, sub-cut (16) 9 1/2" ((16) 6 1/2") squares.
Cut (6) 5" ((5) 3 3/4") strips, sub-cut (48) 5" ((48) 3 3/4") squares; cut each square diagonally in both directions for (192) 1/4-square triangles.

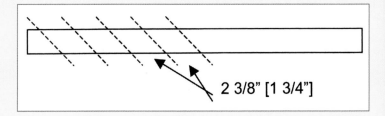

From gold #1 cut (25) 2 3/8" ((12) 1 3/4") strips, sub-cut (192) 45-degree diamonds. Each cut measures 2 3/8" (1 3/4") from the last.
From gold #2 cut (25) 2 3/8" ((12) 1 3/4") strips, sub-cut (192) 45-degree diamonds.

Cut the tip off of each of the diamonds 1 1/2" from the widest part of the diamond if you wish. Since the circle will be appliquéd to the center of the star, you don't need to work with the bulk. In addition, you won't be having to sew the eight seams in the center.

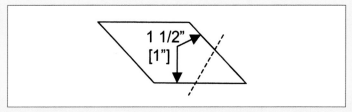

From dark green cut (2) 14" ((1) 9") strips. Cut (16) 1" (3/4") bias strips across the width of the strip for (16) 1" x 19" (3/4" x 12 1/2") bias strips. (You will have leftover triangles of fabric to use in another project.) Use the 1/2" (3/8") Clover Bias Tape Maker to make the appliqué stems.

Constructing the blocks

For each block you will need to make three Lemoyne stars. Each star needs four diamonds from each of the golds. Pair a gold #1 diamond with a gold #2 diamond and sew the short side from the end to 1/4" in from the end of the seam. Press the seam allowance open.

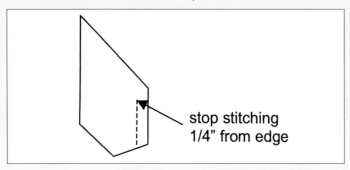

stop stitching 1/4" from edge

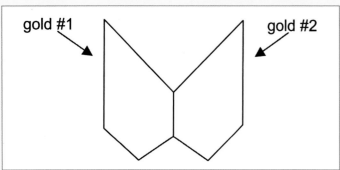

gold #1   gold #2

Sew all the pairs in the same sequence. This way each of the petals will alternate in color.

Each of the Lemoyne stars takes four of these pairs. Set a red 1/4-square triangle into each of the pairs of diamonds. Mark each of the triangles 1/4" from the point.

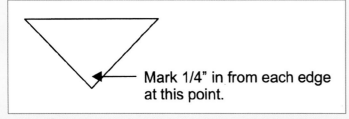

Mark 1/4" in from each edge at this point.

Sew the triangle to the diamond, right sides together, and beginning at the outer point. (I recommend you start stitching on a leader scrap – a small scrap of fabric, folded in two. Begin

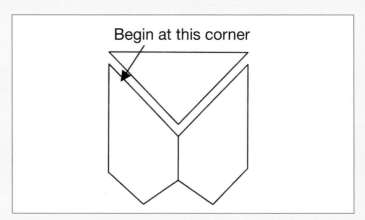

Begin at this corner

sewing the diamonds without removing the leader. This will help prevent the sewing machine from "eating" that narrow point. Also, by stitching from the sharp point toward the side point you will prevent the tip from stretching out of shape.) Backstitch to secure. Sew the other side of the triangle to the adjacent diamond, again beginning with the leader scrap and sewing from the point to the inside corner. You will want to press the seam allowance away from the diamonds, eliminating bulk at the tips of the diamonds.

For each Lemoyne Star, sew four pairs of star points together with a red 1/4-square triangle.

Make a mark 1/4" in from the edge on one corner of the 3 1/8" (2 1/4") squares.

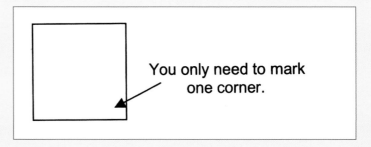

You only need to mark one corner.

Sew a square between two sets of diamond units in the same manner you sewed the triangles to complete the star blocks, beginning at the outside point and backstitching 1/4" from the end of the seam. Sew another two corner squares to the right side of the two halves in the same manner to complete the block. This should provide you with identical, but opposite, sides of the star. Sew the two sides of the star together at these corners. Appliqué the center circles over the center opening of the block. Trim the excess gold fabrics away from behind the circle, leaving a 1/4" seam allowance.

Referring to the appliqué placement guide you'll find with the templates, appliqué the stems and leaves to the 9" (6 1/2") squares. Note the stems extend into the star blocks. Therefore, you will need to leave the stem in the corner free until the block is finished.

Barb used the fusible method of applique. She did not reverse the applique shapes as discussed on page 8, therefore her leaves appear as a mirror image of the leaves in the applique placement guide.

Once the four elements of the block are put together, you will have to open the seam at the point where the stem meets the center flower and insert the end of the stem. Stitch the opening to secure.

Quilting

You have lots of opportunities for quilting designs. Let your imagination run wild. You might try quilting a flower design over the sunflowers instead of outlining each of the star points. Add veins to the leaves and bugs to the background. You have no limits!

Alice quilted an all-over design with curls and petals. It reminds me of sunshine.

Binding

The binding acts as a frame to the quilt. In this case, the binding is 1 1/2" (1") finished. Cut (9) 9 1/4" ((6) 6") strips and sew end to end (following the instructions on page 11), for a continuous strip. I recommend a bias seam, pressing the seam allowances open to eliminate bulk.

Fold the strip in half, the length of the strip, with wrong side in, and press. Attach the binding as you usually do, mitering the corners, sewing with a 1 1/2" (1") seam allowance instead of the normal 1/4" seam allowance. Turn the folded edge to the back and hand stitch to the back of the quilt taking care to cover the machine stitching. Stitch the corner miters closed, front and back.

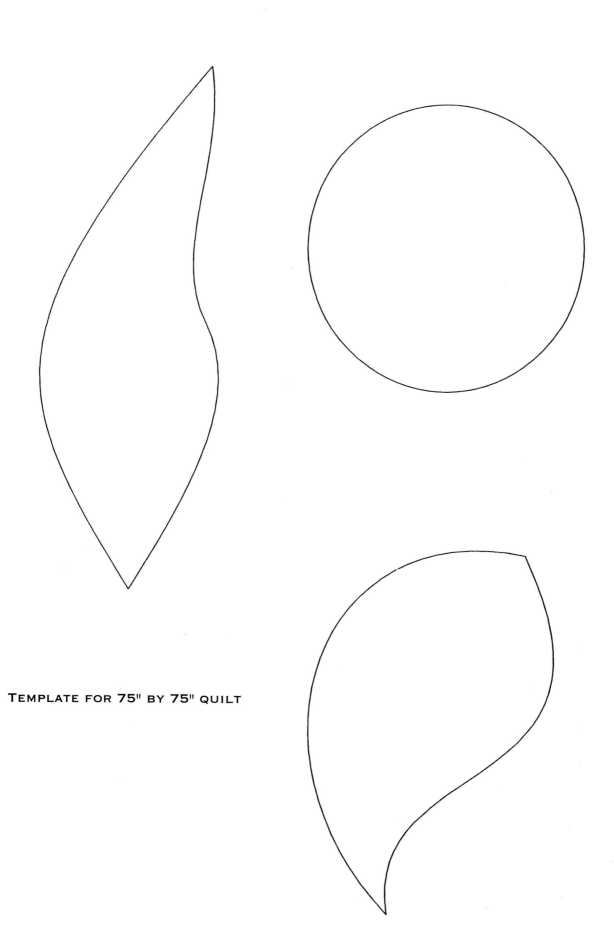

TEMPLATE FOR 75" BY 75" QUILT

STEM FOR 75" BY 75" QUILT

TEMPLATE FOR 50" BY 50" QUILT

73

WILDFLOWERS • 80" x 98"
Made by Kelly Ashton, Overland Park, Ks.

My favorite thing to do in the whole world is appliqué, followed closely by teaching quilters to appliqué. My preferred method is needleturn appliqué; however, to make this quilt, I recommend fusible machine appliqué. I think it would be quite tedious to hand stitch 80 identical blocks. The template provided does not include seam allowance on the curved, or appliquéd, edge, so if you decide to appliqué by hand, be sure to add it to the curved edge only. If you want your quilt to be soft and pliable, I suggest employing the "window" method of fusible appliqué as described on page 8.

Fabric

6 1/4 yards background
1/4 yard each of (16) different prints
For best effect, they should contrast with your background fabric.
3/4 yard for binding
6 yards for backing

Cutting instructions

All cuts are across the grain from selvage to selvage unless otherwise noted.
From the background fabric –
Cut (15) 9" strips, sub-cut (60) 9" squares.
Cut 90" of length and remove the selvage edges. From the length, cut (4) 4 1/2" x 90" strips and set aside for the borders.
Again, cutting from the length, cut (2) 9" x 90" strips, sub-cut (20) 9" squares.

From the contrasting prints –
Cut (4) 9" squares from each of the (16) different prints; cut each square diagonally for (2) 1/2-square triangles for a total of (128) 1/2-square triangles. Use the template on page 77 with these triangles for the flower petals.

Constructing the Blocks

Block A

Choose (32) 1/2-square triangle pieces. Using your favorite method, appliqué the flower petal to (32) of the background squares.

Block B

Appliqué the remaining flower petals to the remaining 28 background squares, (2) petals to each square.

Putting it All Together

Refer to the photo of the quilt and arrange the blocks as they please you. The outside edge of the quilt top is where all the Blocks A are placed. The Blocks B are all within the center.

Sew 10 rows of 8 blocks each. Press the seam allowances in opposing directions. That is, press the seam allowances toward the left on the odd rows and to the right on the even rows. When the rows are sewn together, the seams will nestle together nicely.

Border

Measure through the vertical center of the quilt top. Trim (2) 4 1/2" x 90" strips to that measurement and sew to the right and left sides of the quilt top.

Measure through the horizontal center of the quilt top. Trim the remaining (2) 4 1/2" x 90" strips to that measurement and sew the strips to the top and bottom of the quilt top.

Quilting

Kelly treated four blocks as one flower and quilted accordingly. (1) She quilted lots of leaves behind the flower heads (2) but in the flower petals she quilted feathery shapes and included a flower center. Her use of variegated thread added to the excitement of color.

Binding

Cut (9) 2 1/4" – 2 1/2" strips. Sew the strips together, end to end (following the instructions on page 11), with a diagonal seam and press the seam allowances open to eliminate bulk. Fold the strip in half lengthwise, wrong side in, and apply to the edge of the quilt top, raw edges aligned and mitering the corners. Turn the finished edge to the back and stitch by hand to the back of the quilt.

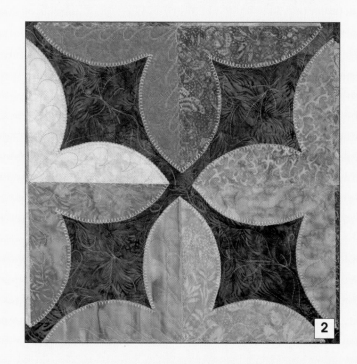

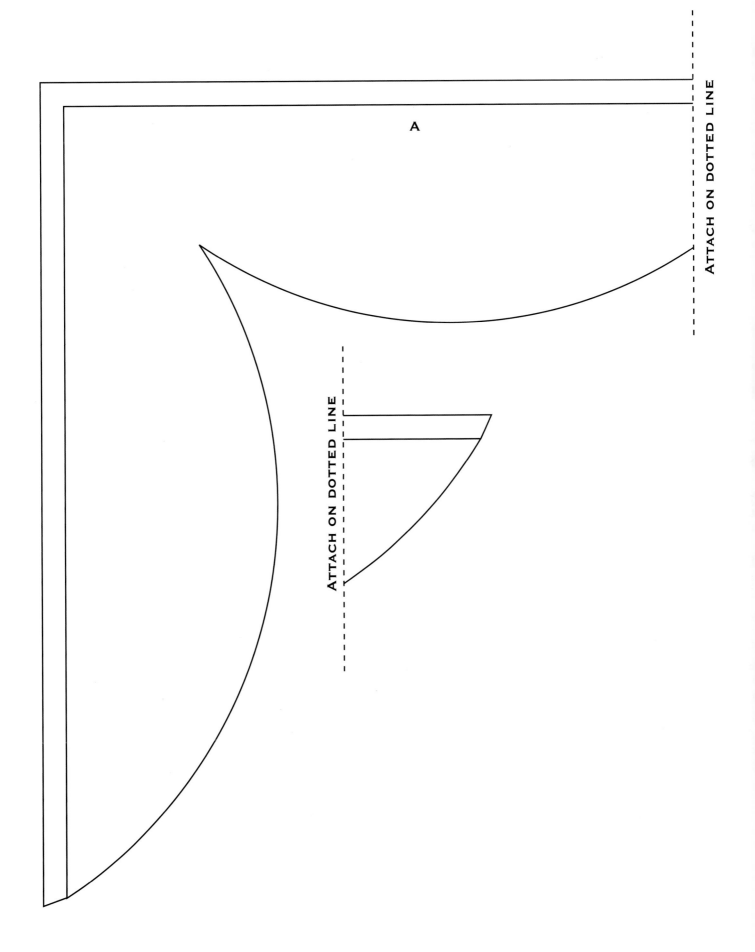

A

ATTACH ON DOTTED LINE

ATTACH ON DOTTED LINE

GUIDING LIGHTS • 42 1/2" by 53"
Made by Kim Morrow, Overland Park, Ks.

Basic Guidelines to Drafting the Mariners' Compass

The more time I spend making quilts, and the more workshops I attend, I realize more and more there is no one and only correct way to do anything. I have also come to realize while this may be true, some ways are better than others. Following is a list of points I feel make the construction of the Mariners' Compass most successful. I am sure there are other ideas out there, but this is what I work with when constructing this wonderful block.

When using a commercial template for a Mariners' Compass block, spray starch onto your fabric and press (both sides) 3 – 4 times before cutting out your compass rays. You want that fabric to be fairly stiff! The starching gives your fabric stability. In a Mariners' Compass, ALL edges are bias! (If you will be drafting your own templates on freezer paper that will stay on your fabric right through the sewing of the seams, you won't need to spray the fabric with starch. Besides, the starch may not allow the freezer paper to stay stuck.)

A revolving cutting mat on ball bearings is an excellent tool! It allows you to rotary cut your fabric without lifting the fabric to reorient.

Construct the star from the outside in.

Construct the block by creating units (think triangles). Two backgrounds and a ray make a unit. (1) Two of these units and a larger ray make a bigger triangle unit. (2) One of these bigger triangle units and a primary ray make a quarter of the block. See how this works? It's easy!

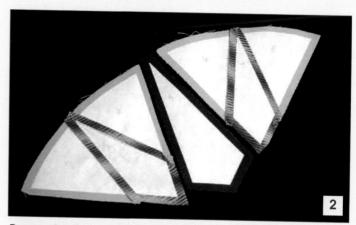

Press, don't iron! Remember, you're most likely working with ALL bias edges!

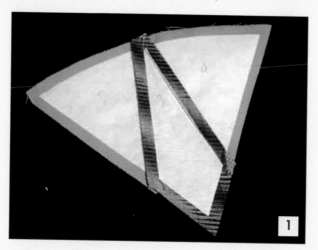

Always press the seam allowance away from the ray point. At some point in the construction, previously sewn seams make you want to press toward the ray. No problem, twist or clip the seam allowance somewhere between the point (where the seam is pressed away from the ray) and the previously sewn intersecting seam (where the seam allowance is pressed toward the ray). (3) Now everyone's happy. Your points stay perfect, your compass doesn't have bulky spots and you have a lovely Mariners' Compass!

Steam and an appliquéd center circle hide a multitude of volcanoes! Don't be disheartened if, after all the care you have taken, you still get that mounding in the center. You probably just pressed too aggressively and stretched something ever so slightly (but a number of "ever so slightlies" add up to a not so dormant volcano). Try steaming out the bulk. You may have to press in such a way that you move the seam line a little. And there is no disgrace if you just cut out the center and finish with an appliquéd circle center!

Drafting Your Own Mariners' Compass Block

The advantage to drawing your own star is you can make it any size you want. You are not limited by the templates, which is why I won't be providing any. I want to empower you to be able to create any style you wish in any size. Draft your star on the dull side of freezer paper. If you plan to make your block larger than 18" square, overlap two pieces of freezer paper and press with a hot dry iron where the two pieces overlap.

Step 1- Establish the block

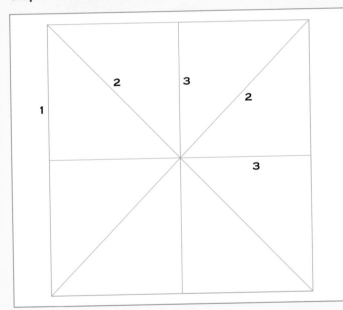

Determine the finished size of the block. Draw a square. (1)

Draw a diagonal line from corner to corner to establish the center. (2)

Draw the "north-south" and "east-west" lines – the skeletal bones of the star. (3) To do this, measure from the side edge to the center point where the two diagonal lines cross. Mark that same measure-

ment on the top edge and the bottom edge. This gives you three points with which your ruler will align. Repeat by measuring from the top or bottom. Mark the same measurement on the side edges so you have three marks with which your ruler will align.

Step 2-Lay the foundation

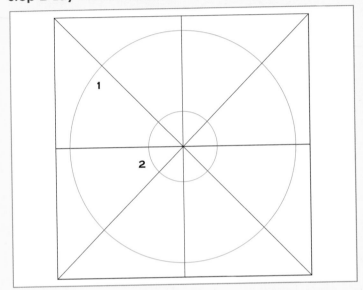

Draw a circle around the center the size you determine the star to be. (1) I recommend the circle be no less than 3/4" to 1" in from the block edge. This will eliminate the normal bulk that occurs, causing the edge of the block to distort.

Draw a circle around the center about 1/4 the size of the outer star. (2) An 18" star would have a center circle of about 4" or 4 1/2". If you make the smaller circle much smaller than the 1/4 of the diameter of the larger star you will have very skinny rays – rather hard to sew. If you have a center circle of much more than the 1/4 of the diameter of the larger star you will have very fat rays.

Step 3 – Primary rays

Always begin with the north ray. Draw a line from the spot on the outer circle where the circle intersects the vertical line (north) to the spot where the smaller circle intersects the diagonal lines on either side.

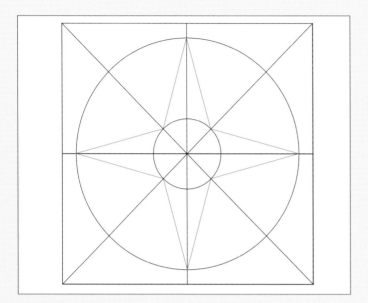

Repeat for the other three primary rays, referring to the diagram here. Notice that each time the point is on a straight line while the base is on the diagonal lines.

Step 4 – Secondary rays

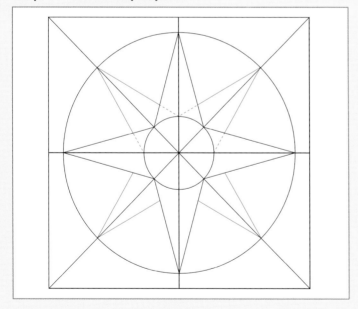

The secondary rays are made the same way. However, this time draw from the point where the outer circle intersects a diagonal line to where the smaller circle intersects the horizontal or vertical lines. Notice each time the point is on the diagonal line while the base is on the horizontal and vertical lines.

In the diagram, I show two styles. You will see two of the rays are drawn all the way to the center circle and two are drawn just to the edge of the primary rays. A line drawn all the way to the inner circle will give you "petals" around the small circle and eight rays that appear to be on the same plane. Stopping the line at the primary ray will give you secondary rays that appear to stack behind the primary rays.

Step 5 – Tertiary rays

To begin you must determine the spot on the outer circle where the points of the rays meet the outer circle. This will be exactly in the center of each of the arcs between the primary and secondary rays. To determine this you must bisect the arc. That is, find the exact center of the space on the circle between star points. Set your compass to be a little more than 1/2 the length of the arc. Place the compass point on a ray point and draw an arc at about the 1/2 mark of the arc. This will be outside the circle. Place the compass point on the opposite point and mark again, creating an X. (See the diagram.) Where the two marks cross is the center of the arc. Place your ruler over the X and the center of the block. Make a mark on the outer circle where the ruler crosses it. Repeat for each of the segments. If you are VERY precise, you may find the star points for half the points. Placing your ruler on the newly found point, extending it through the exact center and then crossing the outer circle on the other side will show you where to make the mark on the other side of the circle. It is advisable that you go ahead and find the center of each segment just to be certain your star is more accurately drawn.

Draw a line from the mark on the outer circle to the point where the second line crosses the center circle (notice the dotted line on the previous page). Stop the line at the edge of the primary and secondary rays.

Step 6 – Decide the style

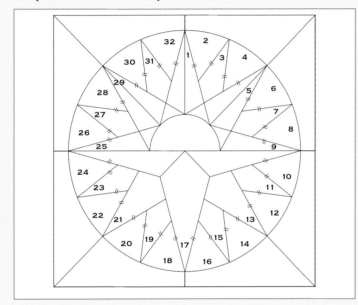

Once you have all the lines drawn to establish the star points, you are ready to determine the style of your star. The lines that are on the paper each represent a seam. So, let's decide which lines to keep, and why.

If you erase the small circle you will have a pieced center. Erase the vertical and horizontal lines and your primary rays will be made from one fabric. (see bottom half above)

Leave the lines in and you can have double sided rays. (see top half above)

Erase the diagonal lines between the outer corners of the block to the inner circle. This will make the secondary rays from one fabric. (see bottom half) Leaving the lines that represent the sides of the secondary rays extend to the center circle you will create a "sunflower" center. (see top half) Have the lines stop at the primary ray and you have a simple star center, whether it is pieced or is a circle. Erase all the lines within the center circle and you have the appliquéd circle as the center of your star. (see the top half of the diagram)

If you draw a line across the base of the tertiary rays you can create the illusion of a circle behind the primary and secondary rays.

Once you have determined the final appearance of your star, mark the templates. Begin by numbering the pieces. The "north" primary ray, no matter how many seams you have in the ray, is always #1. The background wedge to the right is #2. The tertiary ray to the right is #3. The background wedge to the right is #4. The secondary ray to the right is #5 and so on. You will have 32 pieces. If the background wedge to the left of the #1 primary ray is not #32, you have missed something.
Add little "hash" marks between each of the star points and the background wedges. These marks will aid in placement when you begin to sew the star together.

Now you're ready to sew the star.

Constructing the Mariners' Compass
The templates you drafted on freezer paper will be ironed onto the wrong side of the fabric. This means your star will be in mirror image. So if you are going to be fancy with color, remember placement should be opposite to the way you want the finished star to look. You will be using each of the templates in your drafted star. Don't get lazy and decide to use one of the primary ray templates and a stack of 4 layers of fabric (or any of the other templates that repeat). Because you drew this yourself, you may very well have drawn each of the angles slightly differently. If you use all the templates and put them together in the correct order, no one will notice a difference and the star will lie smooth and flat. But trying to use just one of the templates

for all four rays, any differences will be magnified and the star will not go together easily or well. Trust me! You will not be happy.

Press the template onto the wrong side of the fabric with a dry iron set on the wool setting. If the template doesn't stick, it means your iron runs cool, so set the iron on cotton.

Choosing the fabric

The most important consideration when choosing your fabric for the Mariners' Compass is contrast. If you're going to go to all this work, you want to be sure everyone can see it. That means you don't want the points of the star to disappear. So fold your ray fabrics into long skinny triangles and place them on the background fabric. Stand back and squint. Can you still see the points clearly?

Choose prints for the rays that do not include any of the background color. You run the risk of having the star point appear cut off or the appearance of a bite taken out of the side of the ray.

Preparing the fabric and templates

Probably the scariest thing about the Mariners' Compass is the fear of a volcano in the center. This occurs because the pieces get stretched as they are sewn or pressed. All of the edges to your pieces will be on the bias. To give you some help, leave the templates on the fabric as you sew and as you press. If you will be using commercial templates, Plexiglas or some other hard material that allows you to rotary cut your pieces, plan to heavily starch your fabric before cutting the pieces. The starch will help keep the edges from stretching. Speaking of templates: I believe if you have to create the templates by tracing them from the pages of a book or a magazine, you run the risk of having problems. I suggest you draft your own star, creating your own templates, patterning it after the star that has struck your fancy in the book or magazine. Plan to construct just one fourth of the star at a time. The first quarter will include primary ray #1 to background wedge #8. Cut the freezer paper templates apart with scissors or a rotary cutter. (Do not separate the two sides of the rays if you plan to use two fabrics.) As you cut apart the templates, immediately place the template on the fabric you've chosen. This way you won't run the risk of

mixing up the secondary and primary rays. Once you have everything distributed, iron the templates onto the wrong side of the fabric. Unless it matters to the design, I orient my pieces so the straight grain runs through the center of the ray.

If you plan to make your primary rays out of two fabrics, begin by cutting strips about 3/4" to 1" wider than the widest part of half the ray template. Sew the strips together and press the seam allowance open. When placing the template on the strip, align the centerline of the template along the seam. Be sure to place the templates in the same direction so the fabrics will be consistent on the rays.

Iron the templates on, shiny side to the fabric, with a dry iron set on the wool setting. If you find the templates not adhering, set the iron on cotton. Be sure to leave at least 3/4" between templates to allow for seam allowances. Placement of the template is up to you. If I am using a fabric with no directional design, I tend to place the template so the straight of grain runs straight out the point. A directional pattern can be manipulated, though, by the placement of the template. With a rotary ruler and cutter, cut the fabric 1/4" from the edge of the paper template. At the ray points, turn the ruler and cut the point off 1/4" from the tip of the paper template.

Sewing the star

Lay your pieces out next to your sewing machine in order as they appeared before you cut them apart, template up. Constructing the star is simply sewing small wedges to rays to create larger wedges. Do not remove the templates as you sew.

To align two pieces, begin by matching the hash marks on the templates. Match the points in the templates at either end of the seam and place a pin in the seam allowance. It is more important that you align the templates than the raw edge of the fabric. (4) Sew right next to the freezer paper templates, trying not to catch the paper. (5) If your placement is wrong, you can move a template and re-press before unsewing. As long as you still have ample seam allowances all around when you move the template, you're fine and you won't need to unsew. Sew from the raw edge at the point (the outside edge of the star) to the end of the template at the center of the star. If you plan a pieced center, that is no circle in the center, sew the seam to 1/4" from the base of the primary rays. You will be constructing a Y-seam and will need to leave the seam open for that last 1/4".

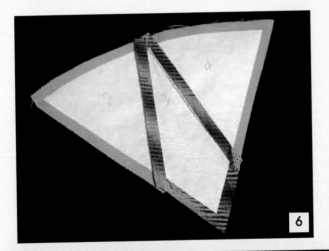

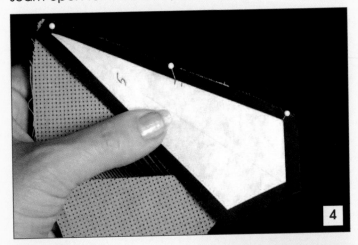

Begin by sewing the background wedges to either side of the tertiary rays. Press the seam allowances away from the point. This creates two larger wedges. (6) Sew these new wedges to either side of the secondary ray. (7) Press the seam allowance away from the point. Notice that in doing so you will be pressing the seam allowance toward an intersecting seam. This will cause bulk and distortion. I twist the seam allowance between the point and the intersecting seam, allowing me to press away from the point AND toward the ray on the same seam. Sew this new wedge to the right side of the primary ray.

When you have completed the quarter, set it aside. After you admire the right side, set it with the template side up on your table, otherwise you will confuse yourself. Only after the whole star is complete should you turn it over.

Now cut the next quarter apart. That is, the east primary ray to the background wedge just prior to the next primary ray. Repeat the above steps for constructing the quarter.

You may sew two quarters together to form a half. To sew the two halves together, sew the rays, leaving the center. If you are going to appliqué a circle in the center, you'll do that last. If the center is pieced, sew the two halves of the center together first and then complete the center seam, connecting the two halves, treating the center as you would a four patch, pressing all the seam allowances in the same direction. (8) Still, do not remove the templates.

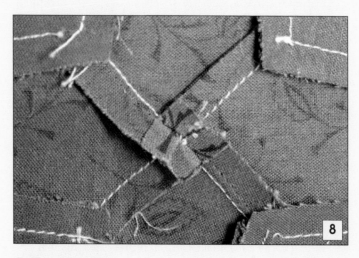

Setting the star

Every pattern for a Mariners' Compass that I've seen has been set into a block that is just about 1/4" (finished) larger than the actual circle holding the compass. If you are like me, you just don't think there's enough background. What usually happens is at the center of the block edges, where the circle meets the narrowest point of the square, and usually a seam, there occurs a bulkiness that causes a distortion and the edges don't remain straight but "dip." You can trim the block to square it up again, but that changes the size. I suggest you always make the background block at least an inch longer on each side to accommodate this distortion. This gives you some room to trim if you like!

I have also found another solution to the problem that opens up a world of design possibilities! What if you want to float your compass on a larger background than you have a template for? What if you want your compass to float off center? You don't even need a template with the following method.

When you have finished constructing the Mariners' Compass, measure the diameter of the circle. I use a drafting compass and draw a circle 1/2" smaller in diameter than my Mariners' Compass measures onto the non-shiny side of freezer paper. I very carefully cut out the freezer paper circle and then

iron it onto the background where I want the Mariners' Compass placed, waxed side down, discarding the extra freezer paper. (OK – I don't really discard it, but use it for an appliqué project later.) Very carefully and exactly as possible, cut the background fabric away from around the freezer paper. Make sure that you mark the North, South, East and West points on the edge of the circle so you can orient your Mariners' Compass correctly. Remove the paper from the fabric and place the fabric circle back in your stash.

Lay the background, right side up, on a table surface. Place the star, right side up, in the center "hole" and align the primary ray points to the marks you made representing North, South, East and West. Fold the background over the star, aligning the raw edges of the circles. Use pins to baste, right sides together, the background onto the Mariners' Compass. When you sew, be careful to only take a 1/4" seam allowance. The only other challenge comes in the fact that you must sew the two together with the Mariners' Compass flat against the sewing surface of your machine. The background is on top. This means that you can't see where the points are as you usually do when sewing triangles to a square as in a Flying Geese block. But if you've been very careful when you constructed the compass in the first place, and if you are very careful to only take a scant 1/4" seam allowance in this step, you will not cut off the point to your rays. Take your time!

It has been said one cannot eat an elephant – it's too big! Of course you can! Just take one bite at a time. The Mariners' Compass is overwhelming if you don't take it just one step at a time. But if you have taken care not to stretch your fabric, have sewn with an accurate seam allowance and pressed carefully, you will be successful.

Drafting an Off-Center Mariners' Compass

If you view life or make your quilts "left of center" you may enjoy drafting a compass that is less than symmetrical. Be sure to have drafted the conventional star, following the directions provided, before attempting the off-center star. These instructions will be clearer if you are familiar with the basics of the Mariners' Compass.

Step 1

Begin by drawing a square at least the size you wish to make your star or larger. This square will be used for measurement purposes only.

Determine the finished size of the star. In this case, we are not going to worry about the "block" but just the round star. Place a dot someplace within the circle, but don't make it too near the center. Remember, this is an off-center star. Around the dot, draw a circle about 1/4 the diameter of the original circle.

Measure in from one of the sides of the square to the dot in the small circle. Measure again in from the same side across the top and place a dot on the line that distance. Repeat with the bottom line. Place your ruler edge on the three dots and draw a vertical line that begins and ends on the outer circle and is parallel to the sides of the square. This is your north-south line.

Measure in from the top to the dot in the small circle. Measure again down from the top on both sides and place a dot on the lines that same distance. Place your ruler edge on the three dots and draw a horizontal line that begins and ends on the outer circle and is parallel to the top and bottom of the square. This is your east-west line.

Step 2

With your compass, bisect the four arcs created by the north-south and east-west lines crossing the small circle. From now on, the outer circle is just the outer limit of the star. Refer to page 81 for directions regarding bisecting the arc. You did the very same thing when you determined the point of the tertiary rays of your conventional star. Remember, though, it is on the small circle that you are finding the center of the arcs, not the outer circle. Once you have bisected the four arcs, use those points to determine the diagonal lines. Draw the diagonal lines, beginning and ending on the outer circle.

Step 3

Draw your primary rays on the north-south and east-west lines, just as you did when drafting the conventional star. Refer to page 80 for directions. Note the rays will not all be the same size because the center small circle is off center.

Step 4

Draw the secondary rays on the diagonal lines, just as you did when drafting the conventional star. Refer to page 81 for directions. Note the rays will not all be the same size because the center small circle is off center.

Step 5

To draw the tertiary rays, you will first have to bisect each of the arcs created by the lines already drawn. If you need to, refer to page 81 again for directions. This time, though, remember, you will not be drawing lines through the center of the circles. Instead, after you find the center of each of the arcs on the small circle, lay your ruler edge so it passes over the center of the arcs and the center of the small circle. Where the ruler crosses the outer circle, make a mark. These marks on the outer circle will place the points of the tertiary rays. Note the size of the tertiary rays will all be different because the small circle is off center.

Step 6

Decide the style of your star. Refer to page 82 for some ideas. The diagram I offer on the next page is a very basic star. It is my opinion that because the star is off-center, simple is better. If you start adding lots of elements, such as split rays (two fabrics) or sunflower center, your star will become too busy and lose some of its impact.

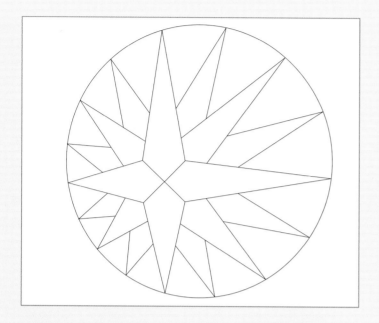

Step 7
Number the segments, beginning with North primary ray being #1. Add the "hash" marks between each of the rays and background wedges for placement while piecing.

Now you're ready to sew your star. Refer to the directions beginning on page 82. It is important to remember the finished sewn star is actually a mirror image of the original drawing. Take that into consideration when making your fabric choices if you plan something like a light source or a graduated color in the rays or background.

Drafting an Off-Center Square Star
An off-center square star is exactly the same as an off-center star, except it is not round. It is square! Please become familiar with the conventional and off-center stars before drawing the off-center square star. The following directions will be easier to follow if you are familiar with drafting the conventional star.

Step 1
Draw a square, representing the finished size of your block. Place a dot somewhere within the square, a little off center. Try not to make the dot sit on what would be a diagonal line drawn through the square. With a compass, draw a circle around the dot. The diameter should be about 1/4 the size of the square.

Draw your north-south and east-west lines as for the off-center star. This time, the lines should extend from the edges of the square. The square will be taking the place of the larger circle in all the stars you have drafted before.

Step 2
With your compass, bisect the four arcs. Draw the diagonal lines beginning and ending on the square. Remember, because the small circle is off center, the diagonal lines will not land in the corners of the square, unless the original dot was placed along a line that extends from corner to corner.

Draw the primary and secondary rays.

Step 3
Bisect each of the arc segments to determine the points of the tertiary rays. Remember, the marks will be placed on the square. Draw the tertiary rays. Each of the rays will be a different shape and size. Don't worry; they are supposed to be.

Step 4
Determine the final design. Again, I think the simpler you make your star, the better. Let the interest be guided by the fact that the star is both off center and square.

Step 5
Mark your pattern as instructed previously. Number the rays and background segments, beginning with north as #1. Make the hash marks for placement as you sew. There is one other mark you need to make, though, that is very important. Once you cut the pieces apart for the square star, you will have no way of knowing which edge of the piece represents the outside edge of the block. The outside edge should always be placed on the straight of grain of your fabric. Without some way to determine the edge, you won't know how to orient your template. Draw straight lines parallel to the edge of the block as in the diagram on the next page. These lines will aid your placement of the templates on your fabric.

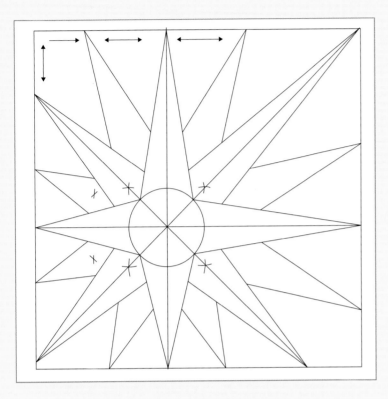

The diagram shows how I drafted the off-center square star as well as the straight-of-grain placement lines.

Step 6
Sew the star, following the same steps as the conventional star.

Now that you have drawn several styles of the Mariners' Compass, experiment with other designs. How about a square star that is symmetrical like the conventional star? The steps are the same as the conventional star. The only difference is that the edge of the square takes the place of the large circle and the arcs that bisected are on the inner circle. Because this star would be symmetrical, you could employ design elements such as the split rays and the sunflower center. You are only limited by your imagination!

Throughout these pages you will see specific tools discussed. Following is a list of these resources so you may find them.

Add-a-Quarter Ruler
    CM Designs
    Available at most quilt stores

Bernina Sewing Computer
    www.berninausa.com

Clover White Pen
    www.clover-usa.com

straw/milliner needles
    www.colonialneedle.com

Triangles on a Roll
    www.trianglesonaroll.com

Tri-Recs Tools
    www.ezquilt.com